Life Goes On

Also by Jeff Jenkins

I Found Him

Emmanuel: God With Us

Easy Street

What Does Grandpa See?

Faith in Focus

Just Happy to be Here

Life Goes On

Jeff Jenkins

This novel is a work of fiction. It includes references to actual events, businesses, organizations, and locales to give the fiction a sense of reality and authenticity. Any resemblance to actual people, living or dead, is entirely coincidental.

Copyright © 2024 Jeff Jenkins

All rights reserved

ISBN # 9798333223258

Prologue

"Hey batter, batter, batter, batter," screamed seven players in the eleven- and twelve-year-old bracket of the Little League City championship game. The two players not hollering were Rick Davis, the pitcher, and Don Thornton, the catcher. Their focus on the job at hand - getting the ball over the plate with the right pitch prevented them from joining in the screaming. The Oakdale Tobacco Company Little League team had won the regular season trophy but now had their hands full in the tournament. With the bases loaded and two outs, the underdog Jones Sporting Goods team threatened to break open the game. Jones was down five to four in the bottom of the sixth, the final inning in Little League. With no at-bats left for Oakdale Tobacco, they could ill afford to allow any runs. One run would tie it, but two would end the game in defeat for the regular season champs. An oversized twelve-year-old, the best hitter on Jones Sporting Goods, waited confidently as Rick prepared to throw the next pitch. The batter, cocky as they come, put his bat over the meat of the plate, looked directly at Rick, and said, "Put it here. I'm knocking this one out of the park."

Don gave his teammate the sign for a curve ball. He feared that the bulky left-handed batter would do as he predicted, and the game would end. Rick shook his head, showing that he wanted another pitch. Don extended one finger as he crouched for the pitch, confirming that a fastball was coming. With a count of three and two, everybody in the park knew Rick was throwing his most reliable pitch, the fastball. Even a single would likely be a walk-off hit for Jones. There was no room for error. A ball would tie the game, pushing the momentum to Jones' side and undoubtedly leading to a defeat for Oakdale Tobacco. It was pitcher against batter, mano a mano, at least as much mano as two twelve-year-olds could muster.

Rick reared back and threw the fastball just where the batter called for it. The huge lefty licked his chops as the ball came right down Broadway. With a mighty swing, the lefty swung with the power to send the ball over the fence, into the stands, and the parking lot. But he whiffed it! Strike three. The ball game was over, and Oakdale Tobacco was City Champs. Don ran to his best friend, Rick, and jumped on him, wrapping his legs around the stunned pitcher's waist like Yogi Berra did after Don Larson threw a perfect game for the Yankees in the 1956 World Series against the Brooklyn Dodgers. With all his might, the frustrated batter slammed the bat into the ground, let out words that a twelve-year-old should not know, and sauntered back to the dugout with his head hanging down.

The parents of the Oakdale Tobacco Company team jumped up and down as if it were the World Series. The team sprinted from the field and the dugout and jumped on top of Rick and Don, forming an immense pile of eleven- and twelve-year-old flesh. Rick crawled out from the bottom of the epic celebration with a huge grin covering his face.

After gathering their gear and accepting their City Champ trophies, the entire team bolted to the Dairy Queen, soaking in the feeling of victory with free blizzards that the ice cream store gave to the winning team.

Oakdale United Methodist Church

Sunday Worship Service

11:30 am

"Go now to serve the poor, care for the needy, and search out the lost. Go now in peace, to love and serve the Lord."

Pastor Don Thornton delivered a powerful message this beautiful fall day to a small but dedicated Oakdale United Methodist Church congregation. He shouted, pleaded, quoted scripture, and brought home the message with his uncanny oratory skills that this older but God-loving congregation soaked in like molasses on a hot biscuit.

"I enjoyed the sermon," said one after another as they marched out the front door, checking their watches to ensure that the notoriously long-winded preacher had not gone on too long. The SPRC (Staff Parrish Relationship Committee) brought this up at their last meeting. They relayed the feelings of a handful of members who wanted to get to the best Sunday buffet in town before the Baptist Church attendees scooped up all the tables.

Dr. Rick Davis, a well-respected physician in town and also the representative to the U.S. Congress, tallied, shaking hands and talking to just about everyone before he made it to the vestibule where Pastor Thornton camped.

With a big grin and a hardy handshake, Congressman Davis reinforced the message just preached. "Great sermon, Pastor. We all need to be more mindful of the needy."

"Thank you, Congressman. I'm glad you could attend today. How long are you in town?"

"Oh, I need to return to Washington tomorrow before the next session starts at noon. We have a packed agenda with the border issue, abortion, and continuing to support our friends in Israel. I'm also doing what I can to keep the filth out of the schools that some of my colleagues keep trying to infiltrate our students with their mind-warping books. Keep praying for me, Pastor; we'll get it done."

"Thank God for Christian representatives like you, sir. Those woke characters are ruining our country."

"I agree. We'll keep fighting. Good afternoon to you and please say hello to your lovely wife. She slipped out the side door before I could speak to her."

"Will do. Have a good afternoon." The lifelong friends parted ways.

The Café

11:45 am

"Here, we saved you and Christina a seat, pastor." Christina, married to Pastor Thornton for eleven years, is a good fifteen years younger than the esteemed pastor. She plays the piano at the church and leads the music, like many pastor's wives in small, low-budget churches. Had she not been a pastor's wife, she may have been a governor's wife, doctor, or lawyer's wife. She dressed conservatively, but her stunning beauty and firm, trim figure turned heads everywhere she went. On Sundays, she strolls like a movie star when she "dresses up" and puts on extra makeup. Indeed, she is a star in little Oakdale, not because of her brain or work ethic, but because of her looks. Christina was cordial enough but never bonded with any of the church's women. She intimidated them with her presence. As soon as Pastor Don and Christina arrived at the table, the eight other churchgoers who meet at The Café every Sunday went off to the buffet line. Christina picked over the salad bar, returning with a small plate of rabbit food. Pastor Don started with a sizeable piece of fried chicken, a heaping spoonful of chopped pork barbeque, collards, butter beans, slaw, Brunswick stew, and also toted back to the table four hushpuppies and a bowl of banana pudding. In a weak effort to cut his losses, he asked the server to bring him a Diet Coke. After the pastor blessed the food, the Methodists dug in, devouring their country-cooked lunch and enjoying every bite. The table talk started with the congregation telling the pastor what a wonderful sermon he had preached, followed by the community news. One Methodist lady started it off, "Miss Viola, after her second, maybe third glass of wine (for medicinal purposes only), tripped on the telephone landline cord and stayed on the floor for over an hour before she realized she should push the Lifeline button her children required her to wear. The EMTs arrived quickly and helped her to her bed with no apparent injuries."

Another regular chipped in, "The young, divorced boy who lives next to me did not come home again last night. I don't know why he keeps that house; he rarely stays home unless his two kids are with him."

"It was nice to see Congressman Davis at worship with us today. He's such a fine example for our country. We need more devout Christians like him in Washington."

"Did you see that those woke crazies in Washington want to allow transgender kids to take part in sports? It's disgusting."

"I noticed the other night that even in our small town, there is a group of blacks and Hispanics sleeping under the overpass. You'd think that the mayor would get them out of here."

After consuming the last bites of The Café's famous homemade banana pudding, with the local news exhausted and the country's problems solved, the group headed home to their couches. As usual, one congregant grabbed the pastor's check with no resistance from Pastor Don. Once again, heads turned as Christina sashayed out of the building.

Cannon House Office Building

Washington, DC

Monday Noon

After an uneventful drive back to Washington Sunday afternoon, Congressman Davis entered his office Monday to find his staff scurrying about, punching keyboards on their computers, talking on their phones, and busy doing whatever folks in a congressman's office do. Rick spoke to them all, smiling, as he sought Eric Bumgarner, his Chief of Staff. "Hey Eric, did you have an enjoyable break?"

"Yes, sir, how about you?"

"Yeah, but I'll tell you. The more I meet with the constituents, the more stupid I believe they get. My gracious, I know we're from a rural area with good, hard-working people, but Eric, they are dumb as rocks. What's on the agenda today?"

Eric fired up his phone, found the calendar app, and announced: "Well, at 2:00, you have a group of environmentalists meeting with you pushing for more clean water measures, then at 3:00, we have six vets just returning from overseas for a photo op. Let's see, at 4:00, a group of school kids from our district is learning how government works. And don't forget Saturday, at 7:00, there's a black-tie gala for a Taiwanese delegation looking to put an ultramodern facility in the U.S. to manufacture microchips."

One site under consideration is next to Davis's district and would undoubtedly create hundreds of high-paying jobs for his district's workers.

"Between these appointments, I have a list prepared for you to call to raise money."

"I'll get those tree-hugging hippies out of here in a heartbeat and start my phone calls. This is our priority, Eric. We HAVE to raise money to stay in the office. Our country depends on our party to stay in power, so those WOKE nuts don't run us in the ground."

"By the way, how's Becky and the kids?"

"Eric, I'm glad I have you to talk to confidentially. The truth is, they are worrying the ever-loving mess out of me. Becky's letting herself go, always tired, whining, and complaining about my not being at home with them enough. We talked about going on a family vacation to the mountains this summer, renting a cabin, and just getting away from all the hustle and bustle of Washington. It sounded good initially, but after I thought about it, my gracious, that would be horrible. Who wants to chase after three small children all day? So, no, that will not happen. Anyway, let me look at the list of donors you have compiled, and I'll get a dozen or so calls in before the hippies show up worrying me about the water."

"Ralph, Rick Davis here. Did I catch you at a good time?"

"Yes, anytime is a good time to talk to you, my friend," replied the President and CEO of the enormous phosphate mine in Mr. Davis's district. "I thought I'd give you a heads up that I have a group of environmentalists coming in today, and they undoubtedly will want something from me regarding clean water. Can you throw me a bone?" After a brief hesitation, Ralph responded, "Sure. How about if I announce we will reclaim one hundred acres of wetlands down our way to compensate for the swamps we had to use for digging?"

"That sounds great. I'll come down for a photo op when you announce the initiative to show the voters that I'm working hard in Washington for them. This area that you will reuse to reclaim the wetlands; is it an area that is valuable to you?"

"Heck no. We never intend to touch that worthless part of the earth, but it will sound good."

"Thank you, Ralph. I'll get rid of these hippies in no time and even invite them to the announcement. By the way, we talked a while back about a contribution to my campaign. We sure don't want a left-wing socialist taking this seat."

"No way. We will not let that happen. I'll throw in $100,000 on this cycle. Is it okay if we handle it the same way we did last time? $50,000 to the campaign and $50,000 to your personal account in the Cayman Islands?"

"Yes, Ralph. You're the man! Thank you, and God bless the USA."

Ritz Carlton Hotel

Washington, DC

Saturday

7:05 pm

Congressman Davis climbed out of the limousine alone and entered the luxurious ballroom, looking for the bar and a familiar face—in that order. He found the bar, ordered a Woodford Reserve Bourbon, and looked around. One perk of his position that this country doctor enjoyed was fine bourbon, and Woodford Reserve was his favorite. Open bar, of course. As he scanned the room, he saw the speaker of the House and his wife, so half sprinted to them to be sure that the speaker saw him there. After a little small talk, he moved on. This function was like a Junior High School dance where the girls lined up on one side of the room, and the boys camped on the other. In this case, however, it was Republicans on one side and Democrats on the other. Occasionally, a junior high girl and boy may meet in the middle, and the same is true for a Republican and a Democrat, but rarely in either case. Rick found a group of his like-minded Republican friends and exchanged pleasantries, feeling comfortable in their small groups. Ironically, few on either side spent any quality time with the guests of honor, the Taiwanese. Finally, as he sipped on his second bourbon, Rick met an English-speaking Taiwanese, to whom he gave a one-minute elevator speech about the virtues of the North Carolina site. The Taiwanese listened politely but had no follow-up questions and moved on. Rick gulped a larger swig of bourbon and headed to the hors d'oeuvre table. As he reached for a mushroom stuffed with crabmeat, he inadvertently bumped shoulders with a lady reaching for the delicacy. "Oh, excuse me, ma'am."

"No excuse me," she replied. As he looked up from the table, he saw a delicacy of another kind. He had never met a more intriguing, more beautiful woman. She wore little makeup; it was unnecessary. She looked to be 5'11", but with her sexy heels, she towered over the 5'8" congressman. Her dark hair, silky smooth olive skin, slight accent, and beautiful smile were overwhelming for this country boy.

"Hey, I'm Rick Davis, a U.S. Congressman."

"Hi, I'm Aleksandre Wojcik. It's very nice to bump into you."

"May I buy you a drink, Aleksandre?"

"Well, since they're free, sure."

"Well shoot, if they're free, let me buy you a stuffed mushroom as well."

" I think I just bumped into the biggest spender at this affair," she replied with a coy smile emanating from her face. After hustling to the bar to fetch her a drink and to top off his, he asked what brought her to a gala honoring a Taiwanese microchip maker. Her reply intrigued Rick. She worked for a multinational data analyst company, and without explicitly telling him, it became clear that the data included sensitive information at the highest level. Making chips domestically was vital to the national security and to her company. She quickly changed the subject to a more generic conversation about great restaurants in the Washington area. She asked if he was a fan of the opera or other Kennedy Center events. It didn't matter to good ole Rick; he was mesmerized, and just the fact that this goddess of a lady was spending time with him and appeared interested in him was beyond belief. He soaked up and savored each precious moment. His self-imposed limit for drinks at such functions was two, but tonight was different. He strolled to the bar, retrieved his third Woodford Reserve, and brought his newfound friend a second glass of Louis Latour Corton-Charlemagne Grand Cru 2020, a French wine too expensive for 98% of the people in his district and unheard of by 99.9% of the same people.

Congressman Davis stayed by her side the entire night. She was out of his league, but for some reason, she appeared to like him and made no attempt to ditch this slow-talking, now half-drunk lawmaker who had never had an original idea since exiting I-95 and heading to the capital. As the nine o'clock hour approached, over half of the attendees had already left or were going to the door. "Rick," she said, let's go to my place for a nightcap. The night is still young, and there is so much more I want to learn about you."

"Holy moly," he thought. "Go to my place for a nightcap rarely meant go to my place for a nightcap. Is it even feasible that a woman like this would entertain the idea of an intimate relationship with me?" Thanks partly to the alcohol, partly because this woman surpassed his dreams as a young man growing up, and partly because he had not had sex with his wife for over three months, he said, "Sure, let's go." She punched ten numbers on her smartphone, and by the time they eased out not so inconspicuously, a limo waited by the entrance for them.

Inside a Limousine

Riding from the Ritz Carlton to Georgetown

Saturday

9:10 pm

As they jumped into the back seat, it didn't take long for Aleksandre, maybe the most beautiful and desirable woman in the world, to Congressman Davis, to place her hand on his knee and rub the inside of his leg. His thoughts were flying through his head at ninety miles an hour.

"What am I doing? How about my poor wife of twenty-six years, whom I have never cheated on before, not even close? Why had she chosen me from all the debonair men at the gala?" Her hand kept rubbing, slowly and seductively, until all of his doubts, thoughts of his moral upbringing, and love for his wife dissipated, replaced with raw desire. He had never been so engrossed with the prospects of sex, ever.

In Alek's Townhome

Georgetown

Saturday

9:35

Sensing the man's inexperience, Alek gently grabbed his hand and led him up to a beautifully adorned townhouse in Georgetown—easily a three-million-dollar home.

"She must analyze some pretty important data," he thought. As soon as they entered the home, there was no talk of a drink. She gently put her long, perfectly manicured fingers to his cheeks and slowly leaned in to kiss Rick.

"It's happening, it's happening," thought Rick. "I can't believe it; it's happening." Once again, she gently but firmly took his hand, leading him to her bedroom, as she looked back at him, smiling. Not a big grin smile, but a small mischievous one that said, "You in for the most scrumptious experience of your life." And off they strolled to consummate this new relationship.

The sunlight slowly filtered its way through the half-open blinds. Rick heard Alek scurrying around in the kitchen. There was an uncanny amount of noise for an English muffin, coffee, and a small bowl of fruit that she had on a tray slowly coming to the bed. She wore an oversized men's shirt, and that was it.

"Oh my", he thought. "This goddess looks just as magnificent in the morning with no prep work as last night at a formal ball." He took his time eating maybe the G.O.A.T. of all English muffins. It was a Thomas English muffin, just like the ones that he had eaten with Becky tons of times. Maybe because he was in bed with a spectacular creature that made this so good. Rick was in a dream that he did not want to end. When he finished his light breakfast, she took away the tray, eased back into the bed next to him, and whispered, "You ready for round two, big boy?" And yes, he was.

Oakdale United Methodist Church

Sunday

9:35 am

Becky somehow got the three boys dressed for church and entered the vestibule four minutes after the service started. It was not unusual for her to scramble in and everyone there knew that she was raising the children on her own since Rick, the ambitious doctor turned congressman, spent most of his time in Washington City, as the old-timers referred to our nation's capital. She had disheveled hair, the tail of her blouse was untucked in the back, and she was a little out of breath from corralling the three boys aged three, five, and seven. She eased the boys into the family's normal pew as quietly as she could, but everyone at the Methodist church knew that she had arrived. At least she was there, people thought. She had not received her normal phone call from Rick that morning, but she expected he would call after lunch.

Reverend Don Thornton delivered his typical sermon, shouting at just the right times. The volume of his preaching scared the boys, but they stayed occupied with coloring books that Becky brought for them, and they behaved fairly well, considering what they were enduring at their age. Becky bought chicken tenders and macaroni for the kids after the service. She knew that that was not a healthy lunch, but my gracious, she was just trying to survive herself.

Home of Rick and Christina Davis

Greendale Acres

Sunday

12:30 pm

Becky looked forward to Rick's call today in that she planned to have a heart-to-heart talk with him. Her lifestyle with three young boys and no dad was not sustainable. He was missing too much: soccer games, school programs, karate lessons, and simply reading to the boys at night before bath time. She was proud of him for running for Congress, and his desire to make a positive difference for the folks in his rural, poor district. But something had to give, and soon. She was exhausted, both physically and particularly emotionally. Three o'clock flew by on the old-fashioned clock that hung in the family room, so she decided to call him. It was not like him to not call, and she began to get a little worried. He answered on the third ring. He took a deep breath before answering from his couch in his townhouse in Glover Park. He answered the phone with a "Hey sweetie." They talked for ten to fifteen minutes about the boys, their school activities, a couple of house maintenance items that she was handling, and a little about the church service that morning. With that over, it was now her turn to take a deep breath as she emotionally tried to communicate to him how stressed she was, how she was losing control of the boys, and most importantly, how lonely she was. He could not help but compare her whining to the magical evening that he spent with Alek last night. No drama, just pure fun, and passion. But he pretended to listen and threw in an occasional "I understand". But he didn't understand or possibly didn't care. She suggested that he come home next weekend and take the family to their river cottage on the beautiful Seraphine River. Directly across the three-mile expanse of water from their cottage, smoke from the AKE Phosphate mine billowed into the sky. The view of the mine was pretty in its own way. This is the same mine that Ralph Johnson served as President and CEO and is the largest employer in Congressman's district. Rick didn't commit to a trip to the river cottage but promised to check with Eric and see if he could clear his calendar.

Oakdale UMC Parsonage

Monday

8:40 am

Pastor Thornton's wife, Christina sat at the kitchen table finishing her second cup of coffee waiting for Don to come down from his bedroom. "Good morning, Don; how did you sleep?"

"Mostly on my back," joked Don. "Let me rephrase that, smart Alec, "Did you sleep well?" No, not really. I can't get today's meeting with Reverend Al Baker, the District Superintendent, out of my mind. Five of the area United Methodist pastors are meeting with him to discuss the possibility of disaffiliating from the denomination. He wants to solidify our support to stay with the United Methodists. I have to say, though, he has an uphill battle with me and, I suspect, with the majority of our congregation. Clyde Woodruff has already told me point blank that if the church votes to stay with the United Methodist denomination, he, his family, and his checkbook are leaving. He said he cannot be a part of a church that condones gays in the pulpit. And there's many more just like him." Christina, confused, questioned him, "Is it not in the United Methodist Book of Discipline that openly gay people were not allowed to become preachers in the church? And that no United Methodist minister is allowed to perform a same-sex ceremony?"

"True, but dozens of conferences throughout the country are ignoring that. Our conference just this past June adopted a resolution saying that they welcome gay clergy."

"It's getting complicated, so I'm anxious to hear what the DS has to say." Here, eat these pancakes. You can't go to such a meeting on an empty stomach."

"Thanks. Is there any of that pure maple syrup that we got from our Vermont trip left?"

"Sure, I've warmed it for you."

Fellowship Hall

First United Methodist Church

Baysville

Monday

10:00 am

The District Superintendent, Reverend, Pastor Al Baker, opened the meeting by thanking everyone for attending, as if they had a choice. After a short opening prayer, he jumped right into it.

"Friends, we're facing a crisis in the church that threatens our very existence. There's much misinformation on the internet by those wanting to disaffiliate, so my purpose today is to give you facts as best that I know them so that you can share the information with your congregations. They will be able to make a more informed decision if and when they decide to put this to a vote.

First, as you know, Methodists have, since their inception, taken on controversial cultural issues head-on. We opposed slavery, took a firm stance, and rallied for women's rights. We've never been afraid to do what is right as long as it revolves around love and grace.

Second, on a more legalistic note that is on your minds, the Trust Clause requires that any church that leaves the denomination may go, but the real estate stays with the denomination. So, people are free to leave the church and either find another one to attend or build a new church building. They also can buy their current building from the denomination at a negotiated price. This has been the policy of the church since its start. At the last General Conference, however, the delegates decided to allow the local churches to leave AND keep their real estate. There is a window to complete this, however, and if a congregation does not vote to disaffiliate during this window, the policy reverts to what it has been forever."

"Al, what happens to us if our congregation decides to leave?" asked one attending pastor.

"Then you have a choice. You may stay with the United Methodists, and we will find you another church to shepherd, or you can leave with the church".

"How about our pension?"

"The General Conference agreed to allow you to maintain the pension you have earned at its present level."

"Can we keep our health insurance?"

"To the best of my knowledge, you may keep your health insurance as well, but this is subject to change. I suggest you check with the Board of Pensions and Benefits before making such a huge decision. Different circumstances with each minister may result in different answers."

"The Bible is crystal clear about the issue driving this monumental divide, stated Pastor Thornton. Just read Leviticus 18:22, which says, 'Do not have sexual relations with a man as one does a woman; that is detestable."

Al responded, "Don, we are not here to debate the Bible today. But may I suggest you be careful when cherry-picking Bible verses? A plethora of verses in the Bible condemn divorce except for cases of sexual immorality or adultery. Read Matthew 19, for example, where it says, 'I tell you that anyone who divorces his wife, except for sexual immorality, and marries another woman commits adultery.' As you know, Pastor, the Bible has been interpreted in many ways by different well-meaning Christians. Some believe with all of their being those passages, such as the one you quoted in Leviticus, as being a hard-fast prohibition against homosexual behavior in any form. Others, who are equally well-meaning Christians, argue that these passages are limited to specific cultural contexts and do not address loving, committed same-sex relationships. So, just as we do not interpret the issue of divorce as literally told in the Bible, some also think that we should not be so judgmental with same-sex loving relationships. Personally, I try to prioritize the bigger truths in the Bible that emphasize love, compassion, and inclusion. To close, let me say unequivocally that the bishop has no intention of sending an openly gay person to pastor any of your churches in this area. She knows that it simply would not work and would be unfair to the pastor trying to lead a rural, conservative congregation such as yours. She just will not put a person through that misery."

"How about apportionments?" asked another attendee. "My little country church pays over $20,000 a year in apportionments that go to the denomination, yet we struggle to pay our utility bill. We certainly have no room in our budget to take care of what Jesus called 'the least of my brothers and sisters.' Now I'm hearing that if churches leave, as we all know they will, our apportionments will go up, not down. We're drowning. Will our apportionments truly go up?"

"That's a fair question," replied the DS. "Our Bishop has made it clear that she and the cabinet will make every effort to reduce expenses so that apportionments will not have to go up. We don't know what will happen until the dust settles and we see how many churches have left. The apportionments, as you know, go to fund missions throughout the world, so I hope that we will not have to reduce our giving to missions. But again, time will tell on all of that."

"I know there are many more questions, and you have much to consider, but our two-hour limit is over. Please feel free to call the Board of Pensions and Benefits for clarification before you make your personal decisions. Let's close with a prayer.

> Gracious Heavenly Father, the God of love, peace, and grace, thank you for each of these brothers and sisters in Christ that have gathered here today. Grant them wisdom and Your guidance as they lead their congregation through this turbulent time. Help them to make decisions as You would have them to make and that their choices will be pleasing to You. Give them safe travels home and bless their families and their congregations. In Jesus' name, we pray. Amen"

"Don, will you stick around a minute? I have something to ask you," the district superintendent asked.

"Sure, not a problem." After the others left, the DS asked Don, "Have you talked to Congressman Davis about this? I'm curious about his take on all this."

"I have, three times. He is adamant that our church should leave the denomination. He thinks that the United Methodist denomination has evolved into a liberal cesspool, if I may be so blunt. He doesn't want to take a leadership role in the debate, but he has indicated that his family will leave Oakdale UMC if we do not disaffiliate."

"I'm sorry to hear this, but not surprised. Thank you for being honest with me. Please give Christina my best."

"Thank you, Don, I will. Goodbye."

The Davis Cottage

Seraphine River

Saturday

9:40 am

Congressman Fredrick Davis arrived late last night, joining his family at the cottage. The trip south on I-95 was more stressful than trying to make a deal in Congress. Drivers are crazy, traffic is ridiculous, and driving at night did not help. But he made it and was glad to spend a little quiet time on the river away from the madness that is Washington, DC. His entire trip down, however, he couldn't look forward to the remoteness of his cottage, the peacefulness of the beautiful Seraphine, or boat riding with his three amazing boys. His mind was unconcerned with upcoming votes, committee meetings, TV interviews, nothing that consumed his brainwaves. He had his focus on one thing: Aleksandre Wojcik, the mysterious, tall, gorgeous, intelligent woman who rocked his world last Saturday night. He continued to beat up himself for one strategic error. Not the mistake of cheating on his wife, not the error of succumbing to her advances, not the mistake of drinking a tad too much that lowered his guard rails and caused him to fall over the moral line easily. No, the significant error that he could not forgive himself was not getting her phone number. He made some inconspicuous inquiries to a few fellow congressmen, but no one took the bait. That one night, better than in his dreams, could not be the first and last time he would see her, or would it? Nevertheless, he was determined to make the best of the weekend and try to get Alek out of his mind for at least an hour or two.

The gentle breeze off the Seraphine pushed with it an unusual odor, an unpleasant one at that. After coffee and a breakfast of fried herring, grits, fried eggs, and a biscuit, Rick and Becky walked out to the pier to enjoy the view, the breeze, and the great expanse of water. The boat traffic was sparse at best. Although a sailor's paradise, the Seraphine was still a well-kept secret, at least nationally. There were always some sports fishermen out, but they did not even see them today. As they reached the pier, the unpleasant odor became foul, almost too intense to breathe. Dead fish were in front of their cottage, all along the shore for as far as they could see. Not hundreds, not thousands, but tens of thousands. They looked like the majority were menhaden, but there also was an abundance of flounder, trout, puppy drum, and croakers. "Rick, that's nasty, what's causing this. This is horrific."

"I'm not sure," he replied. I suspect that some natural causes happen in the river from time to time, maybe low oxygen levels."

"I don't know either, but I can't take this; let's go inside."

Rick had three or four ideas about the cause of the fishkills that he had heard from various environmental groups warning of the degradation of the rivers and that fish kills were like canaries in a coal mine. The dead fish shouted that the river was in trouble and not from so-called natural causes. The problem, without a doubt, was pollution. Pollution in this neck of the woods came from several different sources. But generally, they are bundled into two categories. Point Source pollution refers to releasing pollutants from a single identifiable point, such as an industrial discharge or a sewage treatment plant. These sources of pollution are somewhat easy to identify. The other category is known as Non-Point Source pollution. This pollution originates from multiple, often scattered sources, making it more difficult to trace the origin. Rain carries pollutants such as fertilizers, pesticides, and sediment from various land sources into bodies of water. Poor drainage systems from urban areas are a big culprit. Still, in Congressman Davis's district, it's primarily from agricultural fields that are not utilizing best practices that dramatically reduce this type of runoff. Once contaminants like pesticides, fertilizers, and other toxic chemicals enter a river, they can degrade the water quality, lower oxygen levels, and harm aquatic life, leading to fish kills. Excessive nutrient runoff, for example, can cause algae blooms, which depletes oxygen as they decompose. For whatever reason, thousands of dead fish are washing ashore at the Congressman's beautiful, picturesque riverfront cottage.

Parsonage

Oakdale UMC

Monday

2:50 pm

Pastor Thornton's beautiful wife, Christina, greeted him as he returned from the meeting with the DS, "Hey honey, how was your meeting?" Let me go to the bathroom, and I'll tell you all about it." Upon returning, the pastor sat in his favorite chair, a huge recliner, and automatically turned on the TV, where Fox News immediately popped up. Talking over the noise of the talking heads, Don told his wife, "It's just like I thought. The DS tried to convince us to lead our congregations to stay with the United Methodist denomination. I suspect his job depends on not having many defectors from his district. But honestly, I just can't see it. He knows as well as I do that they are letting queers into the pulpits, and not just in California, but here in North Carolina. I just read online a few days ago that an ordained minister in Chapel Hill married a couple of homos right in his church. It's disgusting."

"But isn't all of that against the policies and rules of the church?"

"Yes, but they're not enforcing it, so there might as well not be any rules at all. It's done, whatever you want, whenever you want, and no one cares. The only thing these jerks care about is collecting the apportionments from us local churches so these hot shots can have huge salaries, luxurious office suites, and lavish expense accounts. I'm sick of it. Our country is going to pot, and the church is going down with it. They no longer follow the Bible. It's disgusting." Pastor Don eased out of his huge recliner, walked to the kitchen where he poured himself a large bourbon, and slid back into the comfortable, well-worn chair that over time had transformed into a perfectly formed cushion for his backside. He took the remote, increased the volume as he listened to every word on Fox, and sipped his drink. After a few minutes of unwinding from his stressful meeting and the fear that is such a real factor in the unknown, Don, in a more optimistic tone told his wife, "The good news is that if our church leaves, and we go with them, we will be able to keep our pension as well as our health insurance."

"Well, that is good news," Christina replied.

Don fell into a mellow half-sleep from the effects of the bourbon and the magical powers of his form-fitted recliner when he heard his esteemed church member and U.S. Congressman, Dr. Rick Davis, on Fox News. "I am proud to announce that I have introduced a bill today that will cut federal funding entirely from any medical school, PA school, nursing school, or any medical-associated field of study if the college or university operates a DEI department, (DEI, or diversity, equity, and inclusion), is watering down the quality of our students in the medical field. Certainly, everyone will agree that when they, or their loved one, go to a medical facility, they want the best possible care. If we focus on diversity instead of quality, people will suffer, and people will die due to a lack of quality, well-trained medical personnel. We cannot let this happen and that is why I introduced this bipartisan bill." The Fox News anchor, trying to look unbiased, followed up with, "Congressman, your critics will say that DEI allows for new perspectives, equity creates a fair environment and can help provide opportunities for those who are not privileged, and inclusion helps these people feel a sense of belonging."

"I went to medical school" replied the congressman, "and believe me, if you do the work, regardless of your color, you will belong."

"Thank you, Congressman Davis of North Carolina, and thank you for your service."

" Chris, did you hear that?"

"What" came back a shout from the kitchen as she entered the family room. "Thank God for lawmakers like Rick. He was just on Fox News. The crazies are admitting gays, blacks, Hispanics, Muslims, Indians, Asians, you name it. If you're not a white Christian, you're in medical school or any medical-related school. Finally, we have a man with a backbone who is standing up to this ridiculous mess. And we are paying for it with our taxes. It's crazy. I just can't take it much longer. These people are ruining our country and all that it stands for." What's Rick doing about it", asked Chris. "He's going to cut off all federal money to any of the programs that continue to have DEI departments. Halleluiah, hallelujah!"

Fellowship Hall

Oakdale UMC

Tuesday

7:00 pm

"Let us pray" announced John Brewbaker, Chairman of the Oakdale UMC Administrative Council as he called the regularly scheduled monthly meeting to ordered. They went through the agenda that the pastor had prepared receiving reports from:

Treasurer: The church is paying its bills with little to spare. He confirmed that the giving so far this year was six percent behind budget, yet the expenditures were almost nine percent more than planned. The unexpected roof repair threw a monkey wrench into the plan. They did pay the monthly apportionment payment to the denomination and were on schedule to complete that obligation by the end of November.

Trustees: The roof repair dominated this report along with a lengthy discussion about what color to paint the front door which is showing significant weathering. The discussion of remodeling the kitchen was postponed again until next month. Pastor Thornton suggested that the two toilets in the church need to be replaced. They worked fine, not a problem, it's just that the pastor thought that with the congregation aging we should replace the commodes with two that are taller. The Council also tabled this until next month to see what our finances looked like. Finally, Pastor Thornton brought several items that needed attention at the parsonage. The Trustee Chair agreed to meet the pastor at the house next week and assess the needs.

United Methodist Men: A quick report from the men showed that they have $945 in their account and that it was close to time to cook peanuts again. The peanuts ministry is a way for the men to raise money for causes that they alone decided. Logistics of who was going to pick up the raw peanuts, who would drive to Mount Olive to purchase the empty pickle jars for the peanuts, who would procure additional peanut oil for the frying that was then scheduled to be held the following Saturday at 7 am.

United Methodist Women: The women reported that they decided to scrub the annual yard sale in that it had become too much work. They also reported that they would decorate the Fellowship Hall for the upcoming fifth Sunday luncheon.

Pastor Report: The pastor reported how many home visits he made last month, as well as how many hospital visits he made. Without taking a breath said, "We need to change the telephone number at the parsonage to an unlisted one. I'm getting far too many calls from people who are seeking help from us. They're not church members. In fact, I don't even know most of them."

"What kind of needs are they asking for?" asked Mr. Brewbaker.

"Well, I'm not sure if they just want money for alcohol and drugs, but what their stories are for things like help to pay their utility bill before their power is shut off. Some say they need food for their babies. Others want money for gas to get to work so they won't lose their jobs. But, like I said, I don't know how true any of this is. I sure don't want our money going to feed a drug habit. So, if we change the parsonage number, Christina and I will not have to deal with all of this. They can come to the church and be properly vetted before we give them a dime." Chairman Brewbaker asked if anyone had any thoughts on this, resulting in only one comment, from the Treasurer, Jackson O'Neal.

"We have unused money available for this kind of outreach. We didn't use all that was budgeted last year." One of the attendees suggested that the group think about the request from the pastor to get an unlisted number and address it next month. A consensus immediately occurred.

The last item on the pastor's mind to discuss was the giant elephant in the room—disaffiliation. Pastor Thornton shared his version of the meeting with the District Superintendent regarding this issue. Thornton explained the logistics of the vote, how it would be taken, the required two-thirds of those attending the vote to disaffiliate, and other legalistic matters. He then shared his opinion. "The United Methodist Church, although it is against the Book of Discipline, is not enforcing the rules that we have. They are allowing gays to preach from our pulpits; they are permitting same-sex marriages to occur in our churches.

There seems to be no moral compass anymore within the United Methodists. Anything goes."

"What have other local churches done?" asked Mr. Brewbaker.

"Of the ones who have already voted in our district, the vast majority decided to leave and join the new denomination, Global Methodists. Some left and are becoming independent. I can't think of a single church that has voted and did not leave. Of course, some decided not to vote and thus will stay with the United Methodists. That is what we need to decide tonight. Do we, the Administrative Council, want to have a vote and let the congregation decide?"

"Well, instead of us debating the pros and cons of disaffiliation here tonight, I think we should at least have a vote," said a committee member.

"Me too," chimed the Trustee Chair. John Brewbaker responded by asking for a motion, which he received, and a second. The Council unanimously voted to have a vote. After some discussion, the vote was scheduled for the third Sunday of next month, contingent on the D.S. being available to attend.

The meeting ended with a prayer from the pastor, and small cliches developed as the people meandered to their vehicles. Many stayed in the parking lot for fifteen to twenty minutes, rehashing the disaffiliation issue.

Cannon House Office Building

Washington, DC

Monday 9:45 am

"Good morning, all," chirped Congressman Davis as he entered his office complex. He was in a particularly good mood simply because he was back in Washington, away from the chaos of his household with a frazzled wife and three needy children. His Chief of Staff, Eric Bumgarner, approaches him with a spunky "Good morning, boss. I have a few items to review with you."

"Well, let's bring me some coffee and get to it," replied Rick. "First, here's your list of donors to call this week. The Speaker is pushing this more than ever. He's running around like a chicken with its head cut off, trying to find a direction to lead, but he knows that money is always the top priority. Next, this week is the vote to amend the Clean Water Act of 1972. The Speaker is under tremendous pressure from industry leaders and large agricultural entities to ease the regulations. They say it's way too costly, the regulatory burden is stifling their efficiency, and the permitting processes are slow and lead to unnecessary delays. These are some of our biggest donors, and the Speaker is determined to help out these folks whenever he can"

"Eric, I was at the cottage this weekend, and there was a horrible fish kill. Thousands of fish washed up to shore, stinking up the place. Becky made me promise to do something."

"I'm just telling you what the Speaker said, and we sure as heck don't want to get on his bad side. He'll put you on the House Committee on Ethics if you are not careful, and you'll be investigating your colleagues. A lose/lose situation. Or worse yet, he'll put you on subcommittees, never to be heard from again. Boss, you need to go along with the Speaker on this one."

"Well, great! Please the Speaker or please my wife. What a choice! "Call in Cheryl. She's up on the environmental concerns of the district." Cheryl appears shortly from her cubicle in the Congressman's office suite.

"Cheryl, sit down. I want to hear your take on the Clean Water Act and how it affects the folks in our district."

"I can do some research for you, sir, if you like." No, unnecessary. I'm just interested in an overview for now."

"Okay, first, the Act regulates Point Source Pollution, which is pollution that is discharged from a specific identifiable source."

"Like from AKE in our district?" asked Davis.

"Yes, sir, that's a perfect example. As a result of the Clean Water Act, AKE and others are required to obtain permits and adhere to strict pollution control standards."

"Yes, Ralph Johnson, over at AKE, reminds me of that every chance that he gets. What else is involved?" The Act sets water quality standards for surface waters based on their intended use, like swimming, drinking, fishing, etc. The EPA (Environment Protection Agency) approves these standards established by the states. The Act provides funding for pollution control programs such as the construction of wastewater treatment plants and infrastructure upgrades to prevent pollution."

"Is this funding in the crosshairs due to the bill that is coming before the House?" asked Davis.

"Yes, sir, as well as funding for compliance personnel. They are already shorthanded, and this bill will reduce their numbers even more. Of particular concern is ensuring that the thousands of acres of farmland adhere to the standards outlined in the Act. This non-point source pollution is killing our streams and rivers, but the government is grossly understaffed to address this issue. In our district, sir, clean water is vital for several industries, including tourism, recreation, and fisheries. The Act has helped over the years by setting standards for drinking water quality, helping to protect public health from waterborne diseases and contaminants."

"You seem to be a staunch supporter of the CWA, Cheryl. After reading the proposed bill, do you think I should vote against it?"

"Yes sir, answered Cheryl with confidence. "I'm not up to speed on all the political ramifications of the bill, and I don't know about all the farmers and industries that contribute to our campaign, but from a purely scientific viewpoint, this bill will cause more stress on our waterways, not less. I've heard some of our colleagues state the opposite on the cable news channels, but they are dead wrong. This bill will set back water quality and therefore our local economy decades."

"Thank you, Cheryl. You have been extremely helpful."

"You're welcome, sir. I'm happy to help."

"Eric, before you go on, I need you to investigate someone for me."

"Sure. Who are we talking about?"

"There was a woman at the Taiwanese reception last week who was most intriguing. Her name is Aleksandre Wojcik. She said that she was a data analyst, but there seems to be more to her than that. Will you discretely ask around to see if you can learn anything about her?"

"Sure, boss, consider it done." The fact is that Representative Davis was more interested in reuniting with the seductive beauty. He rarely went fifteen minutes without thinking about her, replaying in his mind that amazing night that he spent with her. She was like no one he'd ever met before. Certainly, no one in Oakdale was even close to her level. He was mesmerized by her, and it was killing him that he failed to get her phone number and that no one answered the door at her townhouse. It was like a dream that had never really happened, and now that he was awake, she was nowhere to be found. Does she even really exist? She consumed his mind, and he could not focus on the work before him in Congress, much less try to keep his marriage and family together.

"Okay, boss. Are you ready for me to continue with your agenda and priorities for the week?"

"Let's get her done." Eric continued to spell out the more minor duties for the week, such as photo ops, ceremonies for the congressman to attend, and various lobbyists who requested "five minutes of his time." Eric saved the biggest for last. "Boss, a vote for aid to our NATO allies is coming up. This vote is guaranteed to upset fifty percent of the fine voters in our district."

"Eric, I can't focus on that right now. Let's save that one for another time."

"Yes sir, boss, just keep in mind that that one is going to be tough, and we need to develop our position and be prepared to defend it."

"Gotcha, Eric, in due time."

Oakdale United Methodist Church

Sunday

10:30 am

The regulars had all filed into the church and found their typical seats. The Hodges always sat on the second from the back pew on the right side; the Allens sat attentively in "their" pew in the front on the left. Others found their pews as they have done for a generation or two. Christina played as the chatter from the congregation continued as Pastor Thornton tried to quiet everyone to begin the service. He made the church announcements such as upcoming meetings and an outing planned by the "Methodist Rovers" to attend a Gospel Sing the following Friday night. Pastor Don concluded the announcements with the news of a disaffiliation vote to be held on the third Sunday of next month after the morning worship. He encouraged all to be there for this crucial vote, as the church was at a crossroads in its long and glorious history. He explained that the District Superintendent, Al Baker, would manage the proceedings and participate with Oakdale's Lay Leader to count the votes. The congregation stood as Christina began playing, and the pastor led the first hymn, "Blest Be the Tie That Binds." Verses 1,2,3 and 5

> "Blest be the tie that binds
> Our hearts in Christian love;
> The fellowship of kindred minds Is like to that above."

> Before our Father's throne We pour our ardent prayers; Our fears, our hopes, our aims are one, Our comforts and our cares.
>
> We share our mutual woes, Our mutual burdens bear; And often for each other flows The sympathizing tear.
>
> From sorrow, toil, and pain, And sin, we shall be free; And perfect love and friendship reign Through all eternity.

This beautiful, historic hymn, written by John Fawcett in 1782, highlights the unity and fellowship among Christians. It underscores the importance of supporting and caring for one another, which extends to helping those in need within the Christian community. Helping those in need is a recurring theme for Pastor Thornton, one that he shouts from the proverbial mountaintop of the pulpit countless Sundays.

As Christina transitioned to the third verse, in walked, quietly and unassumingly, two new folks into the congregation: a young mother with an eight-nine-year-old daughter. They found seats near the back, opened a hymnal, and caught up with the rest of the congregation, singing the last verse. The mom sang in a low, monotone voice with little expression. The girl, however, belted out the words as beautiful as the hymn has ever been sung in that sanctuary. People gradually turned their heads, trying to discreetly look back and see the source of this gorgeous voice. To the shock and dismay of the high and mighty congregants, they saw two people who clearly did not belong. Both were in dresses, but each was somewhat ragged and dirty. Dresses that these church ladies would not have even given to the Salvation Army, much less wear. These dresses would have gone in the trash in these church-going households. The two intruders wore no makeup, and their hair was scraggly, even though it appeared that the mom had at least attempted to run a comb through both heads of hair. It became apparent to those sitting close by that neither had had a bath in a while, in that an aroma emanated from their pew that caused three ladies to put handkerchiefs to their mouth and nose area in a futile attempt to block the stench. Pastor Don did not allow the distraction to slow down his preaching, singing, or passing the plate. When the plate came to these two outsiders' pew, the mom and the girl each put in a one-dollar bill. After the Benediction, the two outcasts quietly walked out, not to a car, but down the street toward the overpass where a small community of homeless people had staked a claim. Small groups of faithful United Methodists stood in the courtyard, appalled by these two ratty-looking females who barged into their service. Talk of their clothes, their smell, and their shabby looks dominated the after-church conversations. Even those who rushed to The Café to beat the Baptists to the best seats could not help talking about who these people are and how they need to speak to the pastor, "We just don't need people like this infiltrating the church." The congressman's wife, Becky, did not participate in these conversations but didn't stand up for the two people either. She looked at the single mom and her daughter walking away, looked at her three children, and thought, "Only by the grace of God…"

Parsonage

Oakdale UMC

Monday

1:55 pm

"Honey, did you notice those two folks in the back of the church today?" asked Christina. "Yes, who were they?"

"I don't know, but the young girl has a terrific voice."

"Well, I had three different people say something to me as they marched out of the service, saying that they sure hoped that twosome did not return. Ms. Elvira said that they stunk to high heaven." It seems Ms. Elvira, an eighty-one-year-old widow, has roots in the church that goes back to Moses. Some people think that the pastor runs the church; others believe that John Brewbaker, the Administrative Council Chairman, runs the church. But make no mistake about it: Ms. Elvira runs the Oakdale United Methodist church. Her husband was a well-respected attorney in town before his sudden death from a heart attack in his late sixties. He, along with her parents and grandparents, is buried in the church graveyard located behind the church. In her sweet façade of a Christian, she works the phones, dominates the discussions at the weekly shawl knitting sessions, and has an uncanny ability to move people to her way of thinking. If she wants the pastor gone, he may as well start packing. Astute new pastors make her home the first to visit when coming on board. John Brewbaker learned long ago that if he had an initiative that he wanted to be passed by the admin council, he should talk to Ms. Elvira first and make her think that it was her idea. Once that happened, the initiative was as good as passed.

"Christina, I sure hope that they don't come back. I don't need to deal with this while facing the disaffiliation vote. Let's pray they stay away." With that, Don eased back to his bedroom, slipped off his shoes and pants, laid down under the covers of his king-size bed, turned on Fox News, shut his eyes, and faded away into a deep sleep, just as he had done for years on Sunday afternoons.

With him out of the way for an hour or two, Christina, unburdened by his dominating ways, had another idea for her afternoon. She quickly and quietly went to the kitchen and, with a conscious effort to make no sound, made a dozen peanut butter and jelly sandwiches and a gallon of homemade sweet tea, and on tiptoes, silently piled the food into her car and slowly backed out of the driveway. She headed straight to the overpass, expecting that she would find the two church guests camped out there with the growing community of homeless. As she grabbed her sack full of freshly made sandwiches in one hand and the gallon of tea in the other, she slowly walked through the homeless community. Just as the two church guests stood out like a sore thumb earlier that morning, this well-dressed church lady with beautifully applied makeup and perfectly styled hair stuck out in this overpass community. Stares followed her every step. She noticed the attention that she was receiving and became a little anxious. What she saw shocked and disgusted her, making her deeply sympathetic. "What happened to these people to cause them to end up here?" she thought. With still no sign of the mom and her daughter, she weaved her way back to the car.

Then, she heard a sweet young voice say, "You sure can play the piano." Christina turned back and saw the little girl approaching her. "Where did you learn to play like that?" asked Mia, the homeless preteen.

"Well, hey there, I was looking for you," replied Christina with a big smile. "I brought you something." Christina handed Mia the bag full of sandwiches and the jug of tea. "Oh my, Christina remarked, I forgot to bring cups for the tea."

"No problem. Mama has a couple in the tent."

"So, where did you learn to play the piano?"

"My dear, my mama had me in piano lessons since I was six years old. She, too, played the piano, and we often played the piano in our home together. I'd play, and she sang; then I'd sing, and she played. I've always loved music and am so happy that I can play at the church."

"I hope to learn to play the piano someday," replied Mia.

"Well, I hope that you can. Share these sandwiches with your mom and whoever else you want to. I hope that you enjoy them. I must go before my husband wakes up from his nap."

"Bye now, church lady."

"Goodbye to you, sweet young girl."

Oakdale United Methodist Church
Monday
9:05 am

"This is Pastor Don Thornton calling for Representative Davis. I'm his pastor in Oakdale."

"One minute, please, Pastor, replied a professional-sounding receptionist.

"Don, you caught me on my way to a meeting, so I'll have to be brief. What's going on?"

"Okay, Rick, I'll jump right in. I realize you do not control the City of Oakdale, but I thought a call from you to our mayor would help. I plan to call him as well."

"What's the issue?"

"We have a growing community of homeless folks camping out under the overpass in town, and it sure presents a bad image of our town to new people coming in.

We had a couple of them come to our church yesterday and stunk up the place. I suspect Becky told you about them."

"No, she hasn't mentioned it."

"All I'm asking of you, Rick, is to call the mayor and light a fire under his rear end to get these varmints out of here."

"I'll do what I can, Don. Maybe I'll get Eric to call first, and I'll follow up if nothing happens. I'm sorry that I'm in such a rush, Don. I need to go."

"Thank you, Rick. I look forward to seeing you when you're back in Oakdale."

"I'll see you, Pastor."

Parsonage

Oakdale UMC

Monday

9:15 am

Becky answered her phone shortly after she dropped off the kids at two different schools. "Hey Becky, this is Christina. Did I catch you at a good time?"

"As good as any these days. I managed to get some toasted waffles into the boys and dropped them off at school. I hope I dropped them off at the correct schools. I'm a little nuts these days."

" Come on Becky, you're doing great, particularly since Rick is away so much."

"We're surviving, I guess. Anyway, what's on your mind?" Becky, I need your help, and I know that you don't have much free time, so this will not be a huge time-consuming project."

"Oh Lord, what's up your sleeve?"

"Becky, I want to help those pitiful homeless folks that are congregating out by the overpass. I went out there yesterday and am appalled at the conditions in which these people are living. Can we meet for coffee so that I can brainstorm a few ideas that are bubbling up in me? I greatly respect your opinions and knack for breaking down a complex issue into bite-size chunks."

"Thank you, Chris, but trying to raise three little ones on my own and being the sweet little Congressman's wife at events here in our district and in Washington, DC has sucked out whatever creativity I once had. But as you know, I have a passion for what Jesus called 'the least of these brothers and sisters of mine', so yes, I'll help. Just know that I have limited time."

"Great! Thank you. Can you meet me today at the coffee shop on Main Street? I promise I won't keep you longer than one cup of coffee."

"Sure, what time?" How about 11:00?"

"Okay, I'll see you there."

"Oh, by the way, I haven't told Don yet that I want to work on this project. He's so consumed with disaffiliation; I don't want to burden him with anything else right now."

"Okay, I'll see you in a little while."

"Bye."

Cannon House Office Building

Washington, DC

Monday 10:40 am

"Boss, we have to get our act together on your position on aid to our NATO partners. The speaker wants to appropriate more funds as long as we can stipulate that the money goes to provide ammunition, missiles, and other weapons of war made in the USA. Some of our colleagues want to tie the money to building a wall on the southern border and beefing up Border Patrol agents, basically closing the border. You've read all the pros and cons; how are you leaning?"

"Eric, I believe that we should help our neighbors as much as we can, and I like that the money will stay here in the country and produce jobs for Americans. We'll need to spin it to our constituents so that they know that this is not some give-away program and that, in the long run, it is in our national interest. We cannot allow Russia to continue its advances because they'll never stop—first one country, then another. There's no stopping their aggression.

By the way, any luck finding out who this Aleksandre Wojcik is?"

"No sir, still nothing. Are you sure you got her correct name?"

"Yeah, I'm quite sure. Don't worry about it; I was simply curious." The Honorable Fredrick Davis was a lot more than curious. He found her mesmerizing and couldn't stop thinking about her.

"Okay, Eric, get working on a statement regarding my position on NATO."

"Will do, Boss."

After easing back into his office, Congressman Davis asked an intern to bring him a coffee. He then settled in to make fund-raising calls, answer e-mails and texts, and follow up on constituents' requests that his staff could not handle. In the middle of his desk was an 8.5x11 inch manila envelope, tightly sealed with tape, with his name on the outside. It must have been hand-delivered because there were no address or postage marks on it. As he casually opened it, peaking inside, his heart dropped, his hands shook, and he turned white as a sheet. He slowly and carefully pulled the contents from the envelope, ensuring no one was approaching his office. He held close to his chest several high-quality 8x10 photographs of him along with his dream girl, Alek. The pictures were far too graphic depictions of him and Alek in embarrassing and compromising positions. A brief note accompanied the photographs that read: "Vote NO for aid to NATO, or your sweet Becky and your three children will find these photographs interesting."

Rick slumped over his desk with both hands holding up his forehead. "Holy crap", he thought. What have I done? What have I done? What have I done?" Rick looked around to ensure no one saw his obvious, desperate body language or the fear that shouted out from his face. "Holy crap!"

Over the intercom, he asked his receptionist to come into the office. He held up the resealed package of life-changing pictures and asked his receptionist who brought in the envelope.

"I don't know, sir. No one came in with it while I've been working."

"Okay, will you ask Eric to come here?"

"Yes, sir."

"Eric, do you know who brought this envelope to me?"

"No, boss, this is the first that I've seen it. Is it something important or anything that I can help you with?"

"No, it's a prank that I think one of my colleagues is playing on me. Nothing really. Thanks, Eric." After Eric left the office, Rick held his head in the palms of his hands again and muttered, "Holy crap."

The Coffee Shop

Oakdale

Monday

11:05 am

"Over here," motioned Christina as she saw Becky Davis enter the coffee shop. Christina had secured a table in the back, away from the young folks who had spread out their laptops and papers on tables along the sides and the front of the shop. After ordering a couple of fancy coffee drinks, Becky reminded Chris that she had to pick up her little one at noon, so she regretfully had little time. "No problem. I'll jump right into it. As you know, we have a growing number of homeless people gathering under the overpass. Several people after church yesterday are getting upset about the impression that they are making on visitors coming into town. Our downtown merchants fear that shoplifting is on the rise because of them. What you don't know is that I went down there yesterday."

"Wait, you went down to the overpass?"

"Yes, I made sandwiches and tea to give to the mom and the young girl who attended church yesterday. I never saw the mom, but the little girl, Mia, was delightful. She appreciated the sandwiches but was more interested in how I learned to play the piano. I don't know their story, what happened to them, why they are homeless, but Mia deserves better, that much I know."

"Well, Chris, I don't know what we can do. I know that the church donates to the soup kitchen. Don't you think that's enough for a small church like ours?"

"Maybe it is, but I hope not. As I walked through the makeshift camp yesterday and looked up close at the people, I couldn't help but think that we could save some of them. Maybe not all of them, but at least some of them."

"I know Don planned to call the mayor today, but he emphasized moving them out. Getting them away from the entrance of our town and certainly keeping them off of the downtown streets."

"After seeing those people yesterday, I think we can do more. I did a little research, and the pros say that the highest priority is finding them a place to stay, even if it's temporary. Maybe a shelter of some kind. We can see how many rental houses are available with affordable rent. Maybe there are programs for rental assistance that we can help secure for them. We need outreach teams consisting of social workers, healthcare professionals, mental health personnel, and law enforcement officers to connect these people with services. Maybe housing vouchers are available for low-income people to help them get off the streets. Our highest immediate priority is to get them housing."

"This seems like a vast project, probably too big for you and me. I thought that the city and state have programs to help."

"They do, but most of these people either don't know about them, don't know how to secure the services, or don't have the skills to navigate the bureaucracy. That's where we can help. First, we need them off the streets and into some place with a roof. Winter is barreling toward us." Okay, Chris, but this will not address the root causes. We must address the long-term solutions, or all of this will be for naught."

"True, so true. I knew you would help simplify a complex problem. Our town and this region need affordable housing, livable wages, healthcare access, job training, and addressing systemic inequalities, such as poverty, racism, and discrimination."

"I love how you have thought this through, Chris, and yes, I'm on board. I will talk to Rick to see what federal programs are available to help. What else can I do?"

"Thank you, Becky. I know you're overwhelmed right now, so really, all I'm asking for now is to go with me and meet with our Administrative Council chair, John Brewbaker, and also pay a visit to Ms. Elvira. You and I both know that if Ms. Elvira is on board, the others will fall in line."

"Arrange the meeting and let me know. Just remember that I have a brief window while the kids are at school."

"Thank you, Chris. I love you for your willingness to help. May we say a quick prayer together before we leave?"

"Yes, please."

"Heavenly Father, you are the giver of all gifts, and today I thank you for our church and Becky and her willingness to put your children before herself. Guide, direct, and lead us so that we can make a positive difference in the lives of people experiencing homelessness in our community. Let Your light shine through us so they can understand what the love of Jesus Christ is all about. It is in Jesus' name we pray. Amen."

"Thank you, Christina. I look forward to hearing from you, and I'll see you Sunday."

"Take care, Becky."

Cannon House Office Building

Washington, DC

Wednesday 10:50 am

"Mayor Duncan, this is Rick Davis; how are you?"

"I'm great, Rick; what do I owe the honor of this call?"

"Justin, I'm driving a little out of my lane here, but I had a request from some town folks to call you about the problem of the homeless folks camping out under the overpass."

"Oh yes, I've had several calls. I'm meeting with the Council and the sheriff tomorrow to see what we can do. Hopefully, we can nip this one in the bud."

"Justin, have you thought of putting them on buses and hauling them to some bigger city with the resources and the will to handle them?"

"No, do you think I could get away with that?"

"I'm not sure, but it seems worth investigating. Most of them are illegal aliens, and apparently, the Governor of Florida has made some progress with this approach. Anyway, do what you can, kind sir, to get these vagrants off the streets. Oakdale is too nice of a town to let these loafers ruin it. I'll help in any way that I can from my end."

"Thank you, Rick. Rest assured, we'll do something to get rid of them. I may see what laws they are breaking, round 'em up, and send them to the state prison down in White County. One way or the other, we'll get rid of this scum."

"Thank you, Justin. I'll see you on my next trip home."

Mayor Justin Duncan's Office

Oakdale

Wednesday 1:58 pm

"Thank you, Mayor, for seeing us on such short notice," said Becky Davis as she and Christina Thornton entered the spacious, plush office of the mayor inside the historic courthouse.

"Anything for such fine, upstanding women of the community such as you. What's going on?"

Christina started, "Justin, we're coming to you as members of the Oakdale United Methodist Church and also as concerned citizens. We are concerned about the homeless people living under the overpass."

"Yes, I'm aware of the problem," Mayor Duncan interrupted. I just talked to Rick about this same issue this morning. We'll bus them out of here, put them in jail, or somehow get rid of them. Most of them are illegal aliens anyway, so I agree with you that they need to go."

Shocked at several levels, Becky Davis jumped in, "You talked to Rick?'

"Yes, just this morning."

"Well, I'll be talking to him shortly. But just to set the record straight, Christina and I have no intentions of being a part of locking up these people or busing them anywhere. Are we clear?"

"Yes, ma'am, I just assumed you wanted that."

"Christina looked him in the eye and said plainly, "Don't assume, my friend. Is that what they teach you at the Baptist church you attend weekly? Have you not read Jesus' words in Mathew 25:42-45?" Christina recited the scripture from memory, staring directly at the now-intimidated mayor:

"For I was hungry, and you gave me nothing to eat, I was thirsty, and you gave me nothing to drink, I was a stranger and you did not invite me in, I needed clothes and you did not clothe me, I was sick and in prison and you did not look after me.

They also will answer, 'Lord, when did we see you hungry or thirsty, or a stranger or needing clothes or sick or in prison, and we did not help you?'

He will reply, 'Truly I tell you, whatever you did not do for one of the least of these, you did not do for me'."

"Ladies, I apologize. I misjudged your intentions. But we have a problem that I need to address. As mayor, I can't let these people continue to camp illegally under the overpass, and I'm sure as heck not going to allow them to sleep on the streets of our beautiful downtown. The trash alone is accumulating, attracting rats and who knows what else. You have to admit that it would have a terrible effect on the business of our local merchants.

"We have some ideas, Justin, but it will take a unified effort from you, the city, the local churches, and the federal government. Are you ready to listen to our thoughts?"

"Yes, by all means. And by the way, we Baptists understand Jesus' words in Matthew just as well as you Methodists. So, let's move on."

Christina started laying out a comprehensive plan that she and Becky had worked on tirelessly since their meeting at the coffee shop.

"First, I think that you'll agree, we need to get these people out from under the overpass. Everybody wants that."

"Yes," the mayor replied, nodding his head.

"Okay, so let's think of where they can go for the short term. Okay, so let's brainstorm possible short-term locations like the abandoned school on Elm Street, the seldom-used National Guard armory, or one of the vacant tobacco warehouses. This is where you can be a tremendous help, Mayor. Keep in mind that we'll need to install some showers and bathroom facilities, so there will be an expense."

"How about food?" asked the mayor. Where can we get enough food to feed all these folks?"

"I think that with the existing soup kitchen and with all the community churches working together, we can provide enough food for the short term. Long-term, we need a better plan, but for now, I believe we can get them food," answered Christina.

"Hold that thought, Major," interjected Becky Davis. "We need to address the problems that put the people there to start with. One idea is to establish some 'Homeless Outreach Teams' that consist of social workers, healthcare professionals, law enforcement officers, and church people to evaluate each case, help connect them with available services, and to provide specialized aid. Once we get the situation stabilized, we can work on more long-term solutions like affordable housing initiatives, job placement into jobs that provide a livable wage, which will require education and job training, improved access to healthcare services, including mental health, and work on prevention programs aimed at preventing homelessness before it occurs."

Christina chimed in with the huge issue of systemic issues such as racism, discrimination, and poverty. Mayor, we are talking about a huge initiative here, but one that, if we do it right, could be a model for small towns throughout the state and even the country."

"Yea ladies, it is huge. My fear is funding. I'm not sure where the money for all of this will come from. Our city budget is tight already."

Becky replied, "Why don't we slow down a little and take one step at a time? The immediate issue involves getting these people under a roof with bathroom facilities and ensuring that they are fed.

"Agreed," replied Mayor Duncan. "I'll work on securing a temporary building and finding some funding for bathrooms, cots, and other necessities, and you can coordinate with the soup kitchen and the area churches. What do you think?"

"We have a plan!" Becky responded with a huge smile.

"Yes, we do," agreed Christina.

"One more thing," the mayor interjected. "Who's going to explain this plan to your husbands? I received calls from both, and they were more inclined to bus them to New York or throw them in jail than to embark on such that we are discussing."

"Oh, I'll handle Don."

"Yeah, and I'll explain the facts of life to my dear Rick."

"Well, let's get to work. Thank you both."

"Thank you, Mayor."

"Thank you, Sir."

Parsonage

Oakdale UMC

Wednesday

7:15 pm

After a typical dinner of pork chops, canned string beans, and boiled potatoes with a slice of store-bought apple pie and a scoop of ice cream for Don (no dessert for Christina), Don headed to the recliner to catch up on the happenings of the day on Fox news. Christina put away the leftovers and put the dishes in the dishwasher before sitting on the couch beside her husband.

"Don, I met with Justin today."

"The mayor?"

"Yes, Becky and I went to his office to discuss the homelessness issue."

"Oh, Chris, I wish you had not done that. I had already handled that problem. There was no need for you to go over there. Did Becky drag you with her?"

"No, it was my idea."

"Chris, can't you just stick to playing the piano and leave this kind of issue to me? I'm up to my eyeballs with disaffiliation and I sure as heck don't need you to stir up anything right now. Listen to me; stay out of this, do you understand? You have no business interfering with this. I even had Rick call the mayor too, so we sure as heck don't need you two women involved. Just stay out of it," he shouted as his face reddened. "Just stay out of it!"

Christina never felt like her husband, the shouted preacher, ever respected her. He seemed to appreciate her piano-playing skills, and he surely walked into gatherings proud as a peacock with his beautiful younger wife by his side. But that's it. Stay out of church business and certainly out of any controversial issues in town. He preferred her to stick with the garden club and book club, but nothing more meaningful than that.

"Listen, you so-called pastor. You preach every other Sunday about looking out for the needy, the least of these, as you say, and now you and Rick are trying to bus these unfortunate souls to New York or even to jail. You're a fraud, and you know it!"

"Don't you dare talk to me like that, you two-bit tramp! You were nobody until you met me, and I will not have any wife of mine talk to me like that. Do you hear me?"

"I hear you, but you're still a fraud." Christina stormed out of the room to their bedroom in tears, slammed the door, crawled up in bed in a fetal position, and cried. The pompous preacher bolted to the kitchen, poured himself a strong bourbon on the rocks, sat back in the recliner, and listened to the talking heads on Fox.

Home of Rick and Becky Davis

Greendale Acres

Wednesday

8:15 pm

Becky's call to her husband went a little better and more civil than her friend Christina's talk with her husband, but the result was the same. Rick sounded preoccupied and not quite in on the conversation. Becky sensed that he was rejected, as if he had the world on his shoulders. She knew the pressures of being a U.S. congressman and the ungodly hours that they worked, so she cut him a little slack. Something was not right, however. He was not himself and requested her to back off the homelessness problem, informing her that he and the mayor were in conversations about it and promising that they would resolve the issue soon. He did ask about the children, but it sure sounded like he never heard her answer. His mind was elsewhere. Becky ended the conversation as amicably as she could, said she loved him, and said she would talk later in the week. Congressman Rick Davis put up no resistance to ending the call. He couldn't focus anyway

Cannon House Office Building

Washington, DC

Thursday 11:10 am

Congressman Davis caught Eric in the hall, cornered him near the employee break room, and jumped right in without bothering to invite him into his office. "Eric, I've made my decision on the Clean Water bill. I feel that I have to go along with the speaker on this one and vote to water down the 1972 bill, so to speak. Get the staff working on a statement like we discussed the other day. Industry and farmers alike find the Clean Water Act of 1972 too costly, the regulatory burden overwhelming, and the permitting processes filled with bureaucratic delays, which stifles growth. Simply put, the Act is not achieving its intended purpose and is a major misuse of taxpayer funds. It's next to impossible to enforce anyway. Say something like the recent fish kills are from natural causes and not from pollution."

"Yes sir, boss, I'm on it."

"Good, thank you."

"Oh, one more thing, Boss. What should we say to Cheryl, who you remember is passionate about strengthening the bill, not weakening it?"

"She'll get over it. It's part of the compromises we must make to please our donors and stay in good standing with the Speaker."

"Gotcha."

"Eric, one more thing. Have someone call Ralph Johnson at EKE to schedule the press conference to announce the reclamation of wetlands that they plan. I want to be there and want maximum press coverage. The people in our district will notice me advocating for water quality and how EKE, a responsible company, is going the extra mile to protect the water in the Seraphine River and the surrounding area.

"Will do, boss. That should be a great photo op for you."

"I'll be in my office with the door shut, so please keep everyone out while I catch up on some things."

Congressman Davis retreated to his office with plans to ponder his predicament with the compromising pictures as well as attend to some routine phone calls, e-mails, and general day-to-day tasks when he saw yet another eight-by-ten manila envelope in the middle of his desk.

"No, please no, not more pictures," the petrified congressman thought.

After double-checking to ensure that the door was closed, with hands shaking, he ripped open the envelope. Inside, on a single sheet of paper, was the following typed instructions:

Dear Congressman Davis,

The following is a list of pending bills in the House in the next several weeks and how we EXPECT you to vote.

We will compensate you for each vote. Do not let us down.

Also, do not inform any of the authorities.

And do not think that resigning from the House will free you; IT WILL NOT! If you don't join in, you and your wonderful family will end up regretting it.

Now full of panic, Rick tried to think of ways out of this mess he had found himself. He was knee-deep in muck and sinking rapidly. He perused the list and the ultimatum that was presented to him. Fortunately, many of the votes dictated were consistent with his plans, anyway. No problem there. The big one still was the vote for aid to our NATO allies, which he felt from the bottom of his being that he should vote for, but these people, whoever they are, are mandating a "No" vote. Others were minor bills, and he could not imagine why these people could even care. Why would anyone not want to maintain the Intrastate Highway System? That was a no-brainer, but the letter said to vote against it.

"What is going on?" he thought. "Who are these people? Why did they target me, a lowly country doctor from the sticks? Are there other congressmen also under the influence of this evil group? Was Alek the bait for them as well? Were others on the take, or were they being blackmailed as well? How are they going to compensate me? Who is putting these envelopes on my desk and why is no one in my office seeing them? And most importantly, what am I going to do to weasel out of this mess? Think man, think. What can I do?"

Rick emerged from the confines of his office, visibly shaken. Eric noticed his ghostly white face and trembling hands similar to a Parkinson's patient as Rick feebly marched to the water fountain.

"Boss, are you okay?" asked the concerned Chief of Staff.

"Yes, I just have a lot on my mind. I'll be alright."

After a small sip of water, Rick, overwhelmed with guilt and furious at his stupidity, staggered back to his office with a plan formulating in his punch-drunk brain.

"What if I test them? Maybe I can pick a small, seemingly insignificant bill and vote against their wishes. Call their bluff. Could this just be a strong-arm attempt from the opposing party to get their way? Holy crap, what am I going to do?"

Representative Davis, not thinking clearly and with no one to talk to, tested the resolve of this blackmailer or blackmailers. In the afternoon session that day, a vote on a minor issue was scheduled- an issue inexplicably on the list. Representative Frederick Davis defied instructions and voted for the bill. Now it's a waiting game.

"Let's see what this loser will do," Rick thought.

Oakdale Elementary School

Greendale Acres

Friday

3:15 pm

The Davis's oldest son, a rambunctious eight-year-old third grader, literally skipped out of school when the second bell rang. School was over for the week, and Ethan had plans to go fishing in the neighborhood pond, maybe play a little football with the neighborhood kids, and play hard with his buddies, making up games as the day progressed. Hopefully, he, his mom, and siblings will watch a movie tonight and order pizza, which is a somewhat Friday routine in the Davis household. He hopped on his bicycle as always and took off for home, six blocks away. He stayed on the sidewalks as instructed, stopped at every crossroads, and proceeded home without a care in the world. As he made his last turn, only two blocks from home, two men appeared from nowhere. One grabbed him as Ethan kicked, scratched, and tried in vain to scream, but with the bulky man's oversized hand over his mouth, not a sound made it to the streets. In only seconds, it went airborne into the back of a nondescript white van, a van that looked just like the ones that deliver Walmart packages to the neighbor every day. Just as quickly, the other man snatched up the bike and threw it on top of Ethan, and both men jumped into the back of the van as the driver sped away. The entire episode lasted no more than fifteen seconds, and no one seemed to notice. Ethan cried, screamed, fought, and tried to open the van door, but to no avail. He was no match for these two burly men who talked with strange accents. Since Ethan would not obey their orders to "Shut up," he gagged him with a couple of strips of duct tape securely over his mouth. His heart raced, and terror consumed his eyes as the sweet, innocent, naïve third grader tried to comprehend what was happening and why. The boy continued to kick and swing at his assailants until one of them, the ugly one with a big scar on his face, backhanded him to where his head slammed against the side of the van, causing Ethan to crawl up into a fetal position a sob, sobbing uncontrollably.

The van made several turns without speeding and always turned on the blinkers. He drove in a manner that brought zero attention to the van as they methodically took the son of a United States congressman out into the country to a small, rented house with no neighbors nearby. The two men grabbed the now-broken Ethan, covered him with a sheet, and quickly carried him inside. After Ethan calmed down a level or two and his heart rate came down to near normal, Scarface ripped the tape off of Ethan's face and explained the rules of the house.

"No hollering, kicking, fighting, or trying to escape. Break a rule, and I break one of your bones. Understood?"

Knowing that he had no choice but to go along with whatever was happening, the terrified third grader, with a headache like he had never felt and a trickle of blood oozing from his hair, meekly replied, "Yes, sir."

Home of Rick and Christina Davis

Greendale Acres

Friday

6:15 pm

In a full-fledged panic, Becky had called every friend Ethan had who lived anywhere close to their house. No one saw Ethan after school other than jumping on his bike and heading toward home just as he does every school day. She called the police, who promised to patrol the area as well. She called the hospital, but there was no record of him there. Her house is filling up with concerned neighbors trying to help, console, and help with the two smaller siblings. She called Rick's cell phone only to get a voicemail message on which she left an urgent message for him to call her. So far, no reply.

"This is not like him at all." She told a friend who had a listening ear. The friend hugged her and suggested that a couple of them search the neighborhood again, looking for any sign of the boy or his bicycle. They just needed to do something. They cannot just sit there. Finally, Rick called back at about 7:00 pm and tried to calm down his hysterical wife so that he could understand what was going on. After a quick, deep breath, she repeated in a loud and disgusted voice, "Ethan never came home from school. He is nowhere to be found."

"Did you call his friends?"

"Yes, you idiot, what do you think I've been doing, playing bridge with my lady friends? I've called the police, the hospital, his friends, our neighbors, and the school. Nothing. Rick, I'm scared. You need to come home now!"

"Okay, okay, let me think. No flights are going out at this time of day, so I'll get in the car and drive home. Call me if you hear anything, okay?"

Georgetown and I-95

Washington, DC

6:35 pm

With multitudes of scenarios darting through his mind, Rick ran to the bedroom, threw a couple of changes of clothes into a satchel, sprinted to his car, and sped away toward home. He was five hours away, but he was a U.S. Congressman and would obey no speed limits. If stopped along the way, he would show his credentials and inform the unsuspecting patrolman that this was an emergency of enormous importance to the government and that he could not divulge any information. Off he went down Wisconsin Ave, weaved through the streets of Georgetown, and navigated over the Francis Scott Key Memorial bridge, bouncing from one lane to the other headed toward the dreaded I-95 South intrastate highway. He prayed for his son and prayed that the traffic in Fredericksburg would be light. Thoughts of an accident that had not yet shown up on the hospital's computer twirled around in his panicked brain. Maybe the kid went to a new friend's house without telling his mom, although Rick knew that this was doubtful for his rule-abiding son. Then, the enormous elephant now living in that same brain began overshadowing all else.

"Could it be the same people who were trying to hijack his seat and turn him into their puppet?" he thought. "Could it be the Russians that have targeted me, a small-town rural country doctor? Oh my God, please, no!"

He pushed the gas pedal down a little further and approached ninety miles an hour as he merged onto I-95.

"I can't believe I made it through Georgetown so fast on a Friday afternoon," he thought. He kicked it up a notch, now approaching ninety-five MPH, heading south on I-95, weaving from lane to lane. So far, so good. The map from the GPS of his Lexus LS showed nothing but green, again almost unbelievable for a Friday afternoon. Rick darted in and out of the traffic, leaving even the most aggressive commuters in his dust, until he saw red brake lights popping on the traffic ahead. A glance at the screen showed the encouraging green I-95 turn red. He slowed down and scrolled down on the GPS screen, only to find the red for the next several miles. An excruciating pace of five to even three MPH ensued. Then, a complete stop. Fredericksburg!

"With all the brilliant people in this country, why can't someone figure out how to keep traffic moving through Fredericksburg?" he mumbled to himself. He forced his way into the left lane from his center lane position, only to see the center lane move. Back in the center lane, he squeezed his new Lexus. Of course, the left lane picks up. "Relax," he coached himself. "Oh my God, what has happened to Ethan? Is this my fault? Please, dear Lord, bring him home safely. HURRY TRAFFIC! LET'S GO!" Back to another lane, he darted.

Finally, he saw the red turn to yellow on the screen. Traffic speed increased to a blazing fifteen to twenty MPH. Halleluia! There's green on the screen, and just like that, like magic in the blink of an eye, the traffic is back to seventy

MPH. There was no sign of an accident, no road construction, nothing appeared to have caused the delay, and nothing seemed to correct it. He just happens. Back to ninety MPH, Rick flies, passing cars, eighteen-wheelers, RVs, and anything heading south.

Thirty minutes or more passed, and Rick drove as if he were at the Daytona 500 until he saw the blue light flashing and a siren blaring.

"No, I can't deal with this now. I don't have time." The patrol officer slowly approached Rick's stopped Lexus and asked for his driver's license and registration. The patrol officer had already seen the congressman's license plate proudly announcing to the world that he was someone special. This was not an unusual sight for the patrolman. He didn't care. No one drives like a maniac on his beat.

"Officer, I'm a congressman, and someone has abducted my son. I need to get home, so please write the ticket quickly and allow me to leave. Please, write the ticket and let me on my way."

After looking at his driver's license, the patrolman replied, "Dr. Davis, I know you're a congressman, and I appreciate your concern for your son. But I cannot allow you to drive like you're driving. You're endangering not only your life but the lives of innocent motorists. You fall in behind me, and I'll escort you to the North Carolina border. I'll have a North Carolina patrolman waiting there to lead you home. Stay close to me, but keep a safe distance. Do you understand?"

"Yes, sir, and thank you!"

Home of Rick and Becky Davis

Greendale Acres

Friday

11:35 pm

Rick rolled into his driveway, thanked the patrol officer, and sprinted into his house, only to find Becky surrounded by concerned and caring friends, Pastor Don and Christina. Becky was crying uncontrollably. She runs to him, embraces her husband, and tries to talk, but her emotions are too overwhelming to mutter a decipherable word. Tears cascaded from her eyes; fluids ran from her nose as she wiped it with an overused tissue.

"He's gone, Rick. He's gone!" she finally mustered.

Rick held her tight as guilt overtook his being. With no proof, no ransom note, no physical sign of an abduction, he knew. He knew that something evil had overtaken his life, and he didn't know how to kill it.

Rick turned to a local police officer in the house and asked for an update. The police officer knew no more than anyone else. The boy simply vanished in broad daylight. Poof, he was gone.

Pastor Don offered to pray, but Rick was not in the mood for prayer. He wanted action, but what? What were they to do?

At approximately 12:05 am, thirty minutes after Rick arrived home with a highway patrol escort, an inconspicuous white van entered the neighborhood. It proceeded to a side street two blocks away from Rick and Becky's house. Quickly, the back door opened. Ethan jumped out and frantically ran through his neighbors' backyards, the yards that he knew intimately from his days playing in this safe neighborhood with his buddies. Dogs barked. Ethan ran harder, straight toward his home. Scarface tossed the boy's bicycle out onto the sidewalk, and just as fast as the van appeared, it disappeared into the darkness.

"Mama, Mama," Ethan hollered as he entered his yard from the back. "Mama, let me in."

Becky, Rick, and their entourage had never heard a sweeter sound than the voice crying from outside. The policeman immediately bolted outside, looking for anything or anybody, but saw nothing but lights coming on in neighbors' homes. Rick opened the back door to see Ethan, with a bloody face from the hands of Scarface throwing him against the van's side panel, race past him and into the loving arms of his mom, Becky. He was safe; he was home. But he felt scared, not because of the cuts and bruises, but because of the emotional terror that an eight-year-old should never have to endure. But for now, he was home, and he was safe.

Oakdale Police Department

Saturday

10:30 am

Rick met with two police detectives and shared the story that Ethan had relayed to his parents as best as a traumatized eight-year-old could. He left school and started his bike ride home. Two white men with funny accents grabbed him and his bike and threw him into a van. One man, who had a large scar on his face, threw Ethan against the van wall and threatened to break a bone each time he hollered, kicked, fought, or tried to escape. They took him to a house out in the country, but close to the school. They offered him food, but he felt too petrified to eat. One man, a third one, received a call, after which they put the boy back into the van, drove to his neighborhood, and let him go. That was it.

The detectives wrote the complete statement, after which they looked at each other as if asking the other one what other questions they should ask. They had nothing. This is an inexplicable mystery, particularly since there was no mention of a ransom or any other apparent motive for the bazaar kidnapping. They thanked Dr. Davis for his report and for coming to the station and promised to work on the case as hard as they could and would keep him and Mrs. Davis informed of any progress. Rick knew they would find nothing, and the detectives did not have high hopes, either. They would, however, start canvassing the neighborhood immediately, hoping to uncover a clue.

Cannon House Office Building

Washington, DC

Monday 9:05 am

Eric, Cheryl, and other Congressman Davis's staff members met for an informal, unannounced meeting. Rick was still at home in Oakdale. Everyone there had noticed something change in Rick's demeanor. He was fidgety, unfocused, short-tempered, depressed-looking, and a mess. He even came into work with his shirt not tucked in appropriately, sometimes without shaving, and was aloft. They were concerned and asked Eric what was going on. Eric didn't know but offered a weak response that the burdens of his job were too much.

"He tries to please everyone and, in doing so, is pleasing no one. He's trying to do the right thing for his constituents, support the speaker, and follow his heart all at the same time, and it just is not working. Does anyone else have any insights?"

No one did, but all expressed concern for their boss and wanted to help, but none knew how. His unexpected dash home Friday night may have something to do with his odd behavior, but no one knew what that was about either. All they knew was that he was a mess and hoped that he would snap out of it soon. The work environment when he's in the office is deteriorating fast, and there were secret thoughts among some that it may be time to freshen up their resumes. Eric, dejected as the rest, broke up the non-meeting and encouraged everyone to return to work.

Cannon House Office Building

Washington, DC

Tuesday 11:10 am

After taking Monday off to help settle down the chaos that was his home, find a therapist for Ethan, and secure greater security for his entire family, Congressman Davis returned to Washington hoping to discover a way, any way, to weasel out of the mess that he found himself. He saw no hope. Upon entering his office, once again, a plain 8.5" X 11" manila envelope awaited him.

"No, not again," he thought. "I can't take any more of this."

He opened the evil one's envelope, only to find confirmation of what he already knew.

"Congressman Davis, never go against us again. And don't resign, or you will not be as lucky as you were Friday night."

He called his Chief of Staff, Eric Bumgarner, into his office, raised the envelope towards him, and once again asked, "Eric, any idea where this came from?"

"No sir, boss. It was here when I arrived this morning with your name on it, so I didn't bother it."

"Okay, thanks, Eric.

Rick pondered to himself strategies. "Should I call in the FBI, or would they just exasperate the situation? Who's leaving the envelopes, and why is no one seeing who's bringing them to the office? Should I tell Becky about the one-night stand with Aleksandre Wojic? How can I protect my family? Why me, a lowly country doctor? Are other members under the influence of this same evil power? Who can I talk to for advice?"

He had no answers to any of the questions. He just knew that he could not continue like this much longer.

In an effort to get back to a regular schedule, Rick called Eric again to ask about the progress he had made in preparing his statement on the Clean Water Act.

"It's ready for your approval, Boss."

"Okay, thanks. By the way, did Cheryl help with this, or is she even aware of what I decided?"

"No, and no. I elected not to tell her yet."

"Well, please tell her we need to get this over with and move on."

"Yes sir, Boss. I'll tell her now."

Rick closed his door, indicating to the staff that he was busy and not to disturb. In only a few minutes, Cheryl, not deterred by the closed door, barged into the Congressman's office, slammed the door behind her, look him in the eyes with anger busting from her reddened cheeks.

"You double-talking, spineless, hypocritical half-excuse for a man. How could you, after all the reasons that I went over with you regarding the positive outcomes of the 1972 law? I don't know who's paying you what, but you're not the same man that I knew when you came to this office. You're nothing but a power-hungry shell of a man who does whatever the highest bidder demands. You're pitiful."

"Wait a second, Cheryl. You don't know the entire story. This law is not working."

"Horse feathers, Rick!" she shouted as she thought she had never called this man 'Rick'; she had too much respect for the office. "If you spoke your mind, you'd be speechless! You're a weak little man with no plan, no vision, no agenda other than collecting money to keep this plush job of yours. I'm so over this. I quit."

Cheryl stormed out, only to return to say, "And you're a lousy father to boot."

This time, she left for good, gathering up a few personal items from her cubicle. Half-running, half-walking out of the building, she did not say goodbye to any colleagues; she just left. Stick a fork in her, she was done.

Rick sat, shell-shocked, not knowing what had become of himself. In addition to the Evil One's takeover of his office, Cheryl just put a tongue lashing on him the likes of which he had never heard, not even from his wife. He secured his head between his hands, slumped over his desk, and held back the tears fighting to explode from his eyes.

Holy Trinity Catholic Church

3513 N St NW,

Washington, DC

Tuesday 12:33 pm

Congressman Davis, a long-time United Methodist, slowly entered the Holy Trinity Catholic Church. He needed someone to talk to, to sort out the mess that he was in. He did not want to open up to any of his colleagues in the House, nor did he have any desire to speak to his own pastor, Reverend Don Thornton. Pastor Don was too close to Becky and the kids for Rick to feel comfortable. Rick knew that it's common for members of different religious denominations to communicate and offer advice to one another, especially if they share common values or if one seeks guidance from another's perspective. While a Catholic father may not have official authority over a United Methodist congressional representative, they could undoubtedly engage in dialogue and offer counsel if both parties are open to it. He needed someone, and he needed him now.

Upon entering the church, doors unlocked, he found a young lady scurrying about with papers in her hand and looking official. He asked her if he could speak to the Father. Rick did not even know his name and hoped that he had referred to the head of the church correctly.

The church employee smiled and replied, "Father Ryan is not here today. He takes the Sabbath on Tuesdays. Is there something I can help you with?"

Congressman Davis, not wanting to say too much to the employee, asked, "Is there another priest working today with whom I can talk? It's a personal matter, and I am eager to speak to a priest."

"Father Sullivan is here. He is the Director of Religious Education. If you'll have a seat, I'll see if I can get him for you." May I get you a glass of water while you wait?"

"No, thank you. I'll just sit here."

Rick feared he may be sitting there forever and thought this was a stupid idea. He resisted the urge to get up and leave but elected to wait for a few minutes. He was desperate for someone to talk to. Within minutes, a thirty-something-year-old boy appeared, smiled, reached out his hand, and said, "Good afternoon, sir. I'm Father Sullivan. How may I help you today?"

Rick thought, "Holy crap, what am I doing here? This kid is barely shaving and calls himself 'Father,' and I'm here seeking advice from HIM? I just as soon have gone to the local Boy Scout meeting and picked out a confidant." But he had come this far. He was going through with it.

"Yes, Father. My name is Rick Davis. Congressman Rick Davis and I want to talk to you privately and confidentially about something. Do you have the time?"

"I have a meeting in thirty minutes, but follow me to my office, and I'll try to help the best I can. May I get you some water?"

"No, thank you, " Rick replied, thinking they were pushing the water around here.

"Congressman, may we pray together before we begin?"

"Yes, thank you."

"Gracious God, As I prepare to meet with Congressman Davis, I ask for your wisdom and guidance. Grant me the patience to focus, the empathy to understand his concerns, and the words to offer guidance and support. Help me to be a vessel of Your love and healing in this session. May Your Spirit guide our conversation and bring clarity and peace to Mr. Davis's heart and mind. Bless this time we share, and may it be fruitful for Mr. Davis's journey of faith and well-being. In the name of the Father, the Son, and the Holy Spirit. Amen."

"Thank you, Father. And by the way, I'm Dr. Davis."

"My apologies, sir. I was not aware."

"No problem."

"So, what's on your mind?"

Rick, a well-respected country doctor, explained that he had been elected to the U.S. Congress and had a wife of several years back home and three wonderful young boys. He also mentioned that he was a United Methodist. That's when the young priest interrupted and said, "I won't hold that against you," trying to put the Congressman at ease so that he could say what he came in to say. It drew a gracious smile from Rick to where his shoulders relaxed, his handwringing ceased, and he felt relaxed.

Not to be outdone, Rick asked, "What does someone have to do to get a glass of water around here?" That brought big smiles to both. They were feeling comfortable with each other. Father Sullivan jumped up to fetch a glass of water, but Rick immediately laughed, saying he was only kidding.

Rick told the young priest the story of his encounter with Aleksandre Wojic, how she was mesmerizing, that he surpassed his self-imposed limit of alcohol, and allowed her to seduce him to going to her townhouse, and unlike another well-known politician, admitted to having sexual relations with that woman. He told Father Sullivan that this was the first and only time that he had been unfaithful to his wife. The priest jumped in and began his spiel about acknowledging his actions, confessing them sincerely, and genuinely repenting for the harm he has caused to his spouse, family, constituents, and the public trust.

Rick raised his hands, palms facing outward toward the priest, and stopped him and said, "That's not all. Two days later, I received some very compromising photographs of Ms. Wojic and me with a note instructing me to vote in a certain way or the photos would end up in my wife's hands." There's more to the story, but this is the gist of it. I made a mistake, and now I feel like someone controls me. I don't know. I'm afraid they will ruin my life if I don't do what they want.

"Oh my, Dr. Davis, this is quite the conundrum. I cannot help you from a political point of view, but I can talk to you spiritually. First, let me tell my assistant I cannot attend the meeting and proceed without me." The father left the room and returned in three or four brief minutes, this time with two cold glasses of water. They were going to need them.

"First, I think you should take full responsibility for your actions and tell your wife. Acknowledge the hurt and betrayal caused to your wife and family."

"Oh, Father, I don't know if I can do that. It would crush her."

"I will suggest what I think you should do as a Christian; the decision is yours. Next, you should seek forgiveness from God, your wife, and others your indiscretions have hurt. This involves genuine remorse and a commitment to make amends where possible."

"Oh, believe me. I have genuine remorse."

"Next, I believe you should seek counseling or therapy to address any underlying issues contributing to the affair and to develop strategies for preventing anything like this from ever happening again. Without knowing you or your wife, I suspect that marriage counseling is in order."

Knowing what he was hearing was the truth, Rick lowered his head in disgust and remorse, thinking he could not do what he knew was right. He just couldn't face his wife with this.

" Next, Rick, may I call you Rick?"

"Yes, please."

"Next Rick. I encourage you to deepen your commitment to God and strive to live a virtuous life guided by honesty, fidelity, and integrity. Part of this is consciously avoiding any situation that may tempt you again. Place your trust in God. Lean on the broad shoulders of our Lord and Savior, Jesus Christ. Know that you are not in this alone, although I realize you feel that you are. But God is with you. He is with you here in this office. He is with you in the House chambers. He is with you at home. He is with you always. Lean on Him."

"I assure you, Rick, that our discussion is entirely confidential. I will not share this with anyone. And you are welcome to talk to me again. Here is my card with my cell phone number. What do you think about what I have said?"

"Father, I know you are right, but I just don't know that I can do it. I need to go home to think and pray."

"Prayer is always the first step. Action must follow prayer, however. May God bless you, my son."

Rick chuckled to himself, thinking that this young kid called him "my son." But what the heck? He is indeed knowledgeable, and the advice is good, even if impossible to carry out.

Father Sullivan prayed again:

"Gracious God,

Thank you for Rick Davis and for the positive impact that he has had on so many through his medical practice. Forgive him, Oh Lord, as he comes to You with genuine remorse for his sins. Bless him, his wife and family, and guide him through this difficult time. We pray that those blackmailing this congressman find You, discover the joy of Your love, and that they too will repent and live a life pleasing to You. In the name of the Father, the Son, and the Holy Spirit, Amen."

Rick thanked the young priest, found his way out, and walked the approximate one mile to his Glover Park townhouse. He was still confused and conflicted, but he appreciated the thoughtful counsel that he received from the baby-faced Father.

Oakdale United Methodist Church

Monday

Fellowship Hall

9:15 am

Christina began the meeting with prayer, followed by a brief update for the mayor on the steps being taken.

"He's working on securing a temporary shelter for them and searching for funding to help defer the costs of building bathrooms, procuring beds and room dividers for privacy. We need to help secure enough food for them in the short term, and we will need to spearhead the effort to establish teams of professionals who can go to the overpass and begin working on individual cases. Once we find a shelter and get facilities installed, the mayor said he will send his crews and clean up the accumulated trash."

Becky, Christina's biggest supporter in the effort, was not present. Since the abduction of her son, she has done little else other than comfort him, protect him, get him to therapy, and try to keep her other two boys in as regular a routine as she could. It became apparent to Chris early in the meeting that she needed Becky's support. This issue was not a priority for most of those present. They seemed to show up only because Christina is the Pastor's wife, and quite frankly, they had little else to do in between book clubs, bridge clubs, hair appointments, and grocery shopping. They sat there nodding their well-groomed heads as Chris talked but offered a few additional ideas and certainly were slow to volunteer to tackle a task.

One lady present, a wealthy woman who inherited a fortune from her dad's immense farm, broke in and said, "We need to establish a committee to go to the elementary school and review every book in their library. We cannot have our children subjected to the lies and un-Christian smut that is infiltrating our schools. I heard that many of the books on slavery do not represent our Southern beliefs. And don't get me started on books depicting boys holding hands with boys and girls hugging girls. It's just not natural, and we and Bible-believing Christians need to do something about it."

Chris interrupted Mrs. Hamilton, a loyal church lady and significant contributor, to say that this meeting was about the homeless and that she should take up her issues with the Administrative Council. Although not appreciating this rebuke, Mrs. Hamilton remained quiet, although her red face gave away her feelings toward Christina. The meeting went on for an hour. Chris closed it with a prayer, and off they went to their comfortable lives, feeling good that they were involved with a do-good project, even if it was only in name. Chris left dejected but not defeated.

Parsonage

Oakdale UMC

Monday

7:15 pm

After a country-style steak dinner with mashed potatoes, gravy, and string beans flavored with ham hocks, Don sat back in the recliner to polish off a cup of homemade banana pudding. Chris opted for a salad topped with salmon and walnuts. Upon finishing the dishes and cleaning up the kitchen, she joined Don in the family room before Don's heavy eyes closed entirely.

"Don, we're moving forward with the homelessness initiative. I had a meeting today at the church."

"I wish you would drop that. It's not your role to get involved. And I can't take on anything else right now. I'm trying to muster up support to leave the United Methodist Church. You know they are allowing homos in the pulpit. And they're letting United Methodist pastors marry same-sex couples. It's against our Book of Discipline, but they don't care. We need to get away from these gay lovers; it's just blatantly against the teachings of the Bible. Let's just let the authorities handle the homeless, and we can focus on what we're doing at the church. I think that Jackson O'Neal, our church treasurer, still sends the soup kitchen a donation every year. That's enough for us."

"Don, we can do more. I can do more. I'm sick of looking pretty and playing the piano once a week. I want something in which I can make a difference, and I think that this is it."

You know they're nothing but druggies, alcoholics, and lazy bums who refuse to get a job. They don't want your help. All they want is money to buy drugs and liquor. And we sure don't want any of them to come to our church. They're just playing us for handouts. I've seen their kind too many times before. Just let it go, Hun."

"I can't, Don. I just can't."

Don fought his eyes, trying to close, but it was a losing battle. Maybe it was the gravy, or probably the banana pudding sent him over the edge and the overweight pastor drifted off to Lala land. Christina shook her head in frustration but remained resolute that she would charge forward with her efforts, with or without the pastor of the church.

Mayor Justin Duncan's Office

Oakdale

Wednesday 9:44 am

Christina answered her cell phone with surprise and joy when she realized that Mayor Justin Duncan was calling.

"Chris, this is Justin. Do you have a minute?"

"Yes, sure, Mayor. What's going on?"

"I have an update regarding the homeless people at the overpass. I cannot secure the National Guard Armory nor get approval to use the abandoned school as a shelter; there's too much red tape on both. I haven't given up, but both will take too much time, and the people in town are pushing me to get something done immediately."

"Well, thanks for the update, mayor. I wish you had better news."

"Wait, Chris, there's more. I talked to Frank Johnson about this. You know Frank, don't you?"

"Yeah, sure, he owns several rental properties around town."

"Yes. Frank said that he has an old plantation house on the outskirts of town that is vacant and that we can use it temporarily until we find a better solution. It has three and a half bathrooms, six bedrooms, a dining room, a parlor, a gigantic kitchen, and an expansive family room. With some quick upgrades, I think our city inspector will give us the go-ahead to use it. We can convert some downstairs space to make-shift bedrooms with minimal effort."

"What do you think?"

"I think that prayers are indeed answered, Justin. Thank you. Thank you. Thank you!"

"One more thing. I have a high school classmate, Ed Murphy, who went into the ministry, but instead of pastoring a church, he and his wife minister to the homeless in Philadelphia. They're having unbelievable success with their 'Love thy neighbor' approach, albeit a tough-love approach. The percentage of their clients that stay off the streets and find a way back into a productive role in society is far better than anything I've seen. I want to arrange a meeting with you, your committee, Ed, and his staff. If we can't meet in Philadelphia, at least we can have a Zoom meeting to help us get off on the right foot."

"Mayor, I love you. And who said mayors are only good for cutting ribbons and kissing babies? You're the best. Please set up the meeting."

Overwhelmed with joy, Chris realized that her 'committee' included only Becky and herself, and Becky had other issues right now. The women of the church who attended her exploratory meeting last week were useless. Still, maybe a Zoom meeting with a minister who is having splendid success loving and ministering to homeless people may light a fire under one or two of them. The Lord has converted people more callous than these pseudo-Christian ladies.

For now, she wanted to make an appointment with Mr. Johnson to look at the house, and she had many stops on her agenda to develop teams of professionals who would meet with the individual homeless people. Chris was exuberant. It had been years since she felt so excited, so full of life, and so needed as she is right now—maybe ever.

"Don will get on board, eventually," she thought. "But for now, full steam ahead."

United States Capitol

House Chamber

Washington, DC

Thursday 2:25 pm

Just as he said he would, Congressman Davis voted to weaken the Clean Water Act of 1972. His district's press and social media were brutal, showing no mercy for his inexplicable act. He had always advocated for the environment, particularly for clean water. What he would tell his wife was unclear, but one thing was clear: he had no choice. The evil one had gotten his attention with the abduction of Ethan, and the financial support that he received from the AKE phosphate mine, both legitimate and under the table, dictated his vote. The farmers' associations, whom he had courted for donations, would feel gratified that their investment in him yielded returns beyond the calculations of their young MBAs. Rick received the cold shoulder from his environmentally inclined colleagues but had no choice. He felt horrible. He had let down his wife and family, who loved the Seraphine River and grew up waterskiing, fishing, tubing, and enjoying the peace that came over them when they crossed the bridge to their cottage there. His vote would not change that at once, but sure as the sun rises in the east, the river quality would deteriorate over time, thanks to him and many short-sighted legislators. He couldn't help but wonder how many other members had been bought or extorted. And why would a foreign, evil power, who he expected was behind the Alex Wojic episode and his son's abduction, be interested in the quality of water in the United States? Maybe it was as simple as anything bad for America was good for them, at least in their twisted, evil minds. This was just the first of many votes that he had to cast, regardless of his personal beliefs or the will of the Speaker and his party. He no longer was his own man; he was the evil one's puppet, and he hated it but saw no way out.

Oakdale United Methodist Church

Sunday

10:20 am

Mia, the homeless child, and her mother, Jasmine, entered the church sanctuary as inconspicuously as possible. Standing near the piano where she would be banging the keys in just a few minutes, Christina saw the pair from the corner of her eyes and smiled with delight. Others in the congregation stuck their noses up and looked away, refusing to make eye contact with these people seeking God's love. Chris high-stepped it to them and welcomed them with a sincere smile. Jasmine quickly told the only friendly face in the entire church, "Good morning. Thank you. We had no intention of ever returning to this hateful place, but the kindness you showed my daughter with the sandwiches and tea made me think that maybe there was more to this place than I realized. Mia seemed to take to you at once, and for that, I am grateful. Few people are kind to her because of how she dresses and the fact that neither of us has access to a shower. We do our best with public water fountains or, occasionally, a water hose that a downtown merchant leaves outside. Of course, they hurry us off quickly. So, thank you."

"I have to start the service now with my music, but find a seat, and we'll worship the Lord together."

"Are you sure that you don't want us to leave? I only came by to thank you. I don't want to cause any problems."

"Come, sit up front near me. You are welcome here."

The pastor glared at his wife as she sat down on the piano stool and, with more energy than she had felt in a long time, began playing "It Is Well with My Soul." This hymn, written by Horatio Spafford in 1873, reassured believers of God's faithfulness and peace even amid life's storms. Its soothing melody and comforting message helped create a sense of calm and readiness for worship.

When peace like a river, attendeth my way,

When sorrows like sea billows roll;

Whatever my lot, Thou hast taught me to say, It is well, it is well, with my soul.

Refrain: It is well, (it is well), With my soul, (with my soul) It is well, it is well, with my soul.

The service went as had so many before this one. Announcements, joys and concerns of the congregation, hymns, prayers, the offering, and a message of salvation through Jesus Christ were all part of the service. The theme that the pastor spoke of often, and the basis for the Christian faith, centered on the belief that salvation comes from faith in Jesus Christ and that His death and resurrection washed away our sins. Pastor Thornton taught this in Sunday school and preached it from the pulpit for years, so he did his normal excellent job speaking with conviction and no notes. He could deliver that sermon in his sleep.

Christina played music as people filed out of the historic sanctuary, one after another. They shook the pastor's hand and thanked him for the message, saying how much they enjoyed it. The pastor, however, did not shake Jasmine's hand or Mia's and did not respond to Jasmine's greeting. No one else said a word to either of the homeless outsiders.

Overpass

Oakdale

Sunday 2:15 pm

Pastor Don and Chris enjoyed a lovely dinner with JoAnn and John Brewbaker after church. Invariably, someone from the church invites them to lunch on Sundays, and they are at The Café the other Sundays. It's hard not to overeat at a setting such as that for a couple of reasons: 1) the food is always amazing because the church member wants to put her best foot forward for her pastor, and 2) no one wants to hurt the feelings of the cook who puts much time, effort and money in preparing an exquisite meal. Vivian prepared what felt like a Thanksgiving dinner with turkey, dressing, gravy, sweet potato casserole, mashed potatoes, collards, congealed salad, Watergate salad, peas and pearls, rolls, and homemade apple pie with vanilla bean ice cream. One does not have to twist Don' arm for him to overeat, as is apparent by his ever-expanding waistline. Christina had more than she wanted but took small portions, so she was not quite the glutton as her husband.

They waddled from the car into the well-kept parsonage; Don found the recliner, pulled the lever on the side so he was in a prone position, and pretended to watch TV. Chris said she was going out for a while and for him to enjoy his nap. He put up no resistance to a quiet house in his state.

Chris felt a little guilty having eaten so much, knowing what Jasmine, Mia, and the others at the overpass were (or were not) having, so she stopped by the Kentucky Fried Chicken on the way to the overpass and ordered an old-fashioned bucket of chicken with all the fixings. Heads turned as this beautiful woman sashayed through the encampment looking for Jasmine and Mia. Folks looked at the gorgeous, out-of-place lady, while others salivated upon seeing a bucket full of fried chicken with the famous eleven herbs and spices. Mia once again saw Mrs. Thornton before Chris saw her and hollered out, "Church Lady, what are you doing here?"

A relieved Christina headed toward her when Jasmine also appeared from nowhere and gave Chris a huge smile.

"I brought you a little something, Jasmine."

"Thank you. You didn't have to do that. You are kind. Are you sure that you belong to that church? You sure don't act like the rest of them."

"I'm sorry about that. They are good people, they're just afraid of anyone not like them. Please ignore their unfriendliness."

"Come over here. I have a few chairs outside of my tent. Sit and eat lunch with us. That chicken smells scrumptious."

"I can't eat another bite, but I'd love to sit down with you for a while."

Mia jumped into the bucket first, then Jasmine, and ate like they hadn't eaten in weeks. After they were full to the gills, Jasmine asked Mia to take the bucket around to the others and share the unexpected bounty. Christina suggested they keep it for themselves, but Jasmine had no part of that.

"We are family here, and we share no matter what."

Christina, embarrassed, agreed with Jasmine and tucked that nugget away in her brain. This is what God's love is. A sophisticated pastor's wife learned a great lesson from a homeless child of God who has nothing but a tent, two cotton dresses, a couple of blankets, and a heart of gold.

Mia left to play with two other homeless children, allowing Chris to ask Jasmine about her story. What happened to her? Why was she homeless? Jasmine was initially reluctant to talk but slowly warmed up to the kind white lady with Miss America looks.

"I never knew my dad, and my mom struggled big-time to take care of me. I later learned that she was an alcoholic, could not keep a job, and was desperate. I believe she loved me and thought that I might have a better chance in life if she gave me up to the foster care system. At least I'll have a place to sleep and plenty to eat. I was eight years old when she pinned a note on my shirt, hugged me, kissed me, and, with her crying voice, said that she could no longer care for me. She waited until I successfully entered the Social Services office before she sped off. I have not seen her since."

"Oh, Jasmine, that's horrible. What did the note say?"

"It said something like 'Hello, my name is Jasmine, and I have nowhere to go.'"

"How old were you?"

"Eight, I think. Anyway, they placed me into the foster care system, and I lived with ten different families for the next ten years. I had such a bad first eight years of life that I thought this may be good for me. And it was. I ate well and had a warm place to stay. The horror of abandonment by my mom is something that I have yet to wrap my head around. I swore that no matter how tough it was, I would never abandon Mia. She knows we don't own any physical things, but we have each other, and I love her and will always protect her.

"Were you able to get therapy through the system to deal with your abandonment issues?"

"Haha, that's funny. They want to place the kids in homes, but to try to get to know us individually and address our needs is not on their radar. I went from a group home to a family, back to a group home, then to another family. I had no sense of belonging. I never felt safe or any feeling of attachment. Trusting no one was my stance, and it stayed the same. I'm not even sure why I'm telling you all this."

"Jasmine, you can trust me."

"We'll see. I hope so. Because I was tossed around so much, I attended more schools than athletes today chasing NIL money. I had no friends, no real help in school, no relationships with teachers. I was only one of those poor, half-white/half-black kids that did not fit anywhere."

"How about Mia's father?"

"Oh, I forgot his name and only saw him that one night. He does not know that he is a dad, and that's fine with me. He was a piece of junk that I fell for in a moment of weakness. I never had a family doctor; actually, I rarely even went to a doctor. I do not know what shots I've had. Never once did a teacher call any of my foster parents when I strayed from academics. I lived alone in various strangers' homes. Don't get me wrong, some of these couples tried, but we just never clicked. I tried at first, but then I gave up. I knew that if I became too attached to anybody, I would experience heartbreak when they moved me from one family to another. Being biracial didn't help me either. Rich white people who serve as foster parents don't want a biracial girl. They passed over me like I had AIDS, or worse."

"So, how did you end up on the street?"

"I had jobs from time to time and picked up various skills, but with a small child, it was difficult. I cannot afford daycare, so what was I to do?"

"How do you afford any food or health care for Mia?"

"I'm an excellent reader because books were my only escape from the horror I experienced. So, I researched government programs that could help people like me. I went to the public library and used their computers to do more research. I even went to the very Department of Social Services building where my mom dropped me off years ago. It's very confusing, but I enrolled in TANF-Temporary Assistance for Needy Families. I received petty cash from them. SNAP, or food stamps, helped a little with food. I was getting help from WIC, but Mia aged out of that. Medicaid helps with healthcare, but again, the red tape will tie you in knots, and I have been turned away from many doctors' offices. I tried Section 8 housing, but so far, I cannot get into any of those places. So, I get just enough help to survive, but nowhere near enough to have an apartment or buy a car. With no car to get to work and no childcare for after school or summers, I'm stuck. I'm just stuck."

Christina looked down at her watch and, in disbelief, exclaimed, "Oh my gracious, Don is going to freak out that I'm not home yet. I have to go, Jasmine, but I want to talk some more. Please come to church again on Sunday. I'm working on something that may help you and the rest of these people here. Please, come to church on Sunday."

"We'll see. Maybe I will. Thank you for the chicken."

Cannon House Office Building

Washington, DC

Tuesday 11:10 pm

The over-achieving House Staff, the micromanaging members of Congress, the lobbyists, everyone vacated the Cannon House Office Building except for the cleaning crew. The man cleaning Congressman Davis's office wore the janitorial company's standard uniform, including khakis, a matching khaki shirt with a company logo on the chest, and a lightweight jacket with the company logo sewn on the chest. He entered the office as always, reached behind his back as if to scratch the small of his back, and pulled out an

8 1/2" X11" manila envelope. Without skipping a beat, he positioned his body between the envelope and the glass windows of the office, then placed the envelope on the Congressman's desk. He continued to clean, empty trash cans, and perform other janitorial tasks as he does every night for several offices. And he was gone, on to another office. Inside the envelope was another directive and threat from the Evil One.

Until now, we have been playing minor league ball. Now, you are in the big leagues. Vote AGAINST ANY aid to NATO members.

AKE Mine

Adamsville, NC

Wednesday 10:05 am

Congressman Davis stepped up to the makeshift microphone at the sight of wetlands that AKE had created to offset the destruction of ancient wetlands by their phosphate mining process. In attendance were several local media people, Ralph Johnson, President and CEO of AKE, several members of his staff, the mayor of Adamsville, the state senator for that district, a couple of local elected officials, and several local citizens.

"Mr. Johnson, Senator Pinkney, Representative Carden, AKE staff, Mayor Peterson, distinguished guests, and members of the media,

Today is a historic day in the life of our beautiful Seraphine River, for our district, and AKE. This fine company employs more people than any other company east of I-95. They inject millions of dollars into our economy annually through their payroll and unwavering policy to buy local and hire local subcontractors. The taxes that they pay help support our schools, highways, fire departments, police and sheriff's departments, and all of our shared infrastructure. In fact, they are the largest taxpayer in my entire district and one of the biggest in the state. AKE is a beacon of light for other companies to follow, as proven by their true partnership with us, the people of eastern North Carolina. They continually do more than their fair share to improve the communities in which we live, and their employees live.

Today, we celebrate the creation of over fifty acres of wetlands created by AKE to ensure the proper filtering of excess water drainage and preserve the precious wildlife that inhabits this significant part of the state. I stand with all the people in thanking AKE as I continue to fight for responsible management of our environment. My entire office and I remain steadfast in forming partnerships with responsible companies like AKE and broad-minded visionary leaders like Ralph Johnson.

Thank you all for attending and commemorating this historic event.

After the mandatory photographs by the media, small talk among the attendees, and three impromptu interviews with local media, Ralph Johnson and

Congressman Davis left in a four-wheel-drive vehicle driven by an AKE employee to join the others in attendance for a locally caught fish fry lunch at the mine's recreation center.

None of the local media personnel knew or cared about the details of what AKE had done to deserve this recognition. They lacked knowledge and interest in the details of what was just celebrated. They chose not to delve deeply into anything beyond the surface, understanding the significance of AKE money to the entire region. The fact that wetland mitigation is required by law as part of the permitting process for mining activities that impact wetlands never came up. AKE did not produce the artificial wetlands out of the goodness of their hearts. It's a requirement. Phosphate mining companies must restore, create, or enhance wetlands in other areas to compensate for the wetlands lost by mining activities. These mitigation efforts aim to offset the environmental impacts of mining and promote the restoration of wetland ecosystems. In this case, AKE met the minimum requirement as dictated by law, and that was only after several battles with state and local regulators. But on this day, the big public relations machine ran to perfection.

After lunch, Ralph and Rick walked alone to the company airstrip where an AKE plane was prepped for takeoff to transport the Congressman back to Washington. Ralph acknowledged Rick's contribution and said, "Rick, I appreciate your help in watering down the Clean Water Act. That's going to be of great help to us."

"No problem, Ralph. You and your company do so much for me and these communities. If I can help, I will. And your contributions are most helpful as well." Rick winked at the CEO when he said this.

"Rick, on a personal note, are you okay? You seem distracted and even a little depressed, if I may be so bold. You just don't seem like your normal, energetic self."

"Yes, I'm fine. I just have a lot of things going on and am a little overwhelmed," Rick lied. "I'll be fine. Thanks for the use of your plane."

"Okay, Rick. Take care of yourself, and thank you for everything you do."

Zoom Call

Ed Murphy – Philadelphia

Christina Thornton & Rebecca Davis- Oakdale

Thursday

9:30 am

After a few "hellos" and a sincere "thank you" from Becky and Chris, as well as a little talk about their mutual friend, Mayor Justin Duncan, the Zoom meeting with Ed Murphy started in earnest.

"So, we've heard so much about your work at "All God's Children" shelter there in Philadelphia," Chris started, "and we've done a little research about your work on Google. What do you think makes your shelter so successful? We're trying to maybe not solve, but at least make a difference helping the homeless people in our community."

"I don't even know where to start, but I will say that we are not 100% successful with all our homeless people, and it's heartbreaking when we lose one back to the street or worse. I can say, though, that our motto is 'Give a man a fish and feed him for a day. Teach a man to fish and feed him for a lifetime' is paramount in all that we do. Soup kitchens are wonderful, and they serve a short-term need. But they do not even attempt to solve the root causes. We try to do that here, based on God's love."

"What services do you provide?" asked Becky.

"Well, we obviously provide shelter, but also meals, healthcare, addiction recovery support, and spiritual guidance."

"This is overwhelming. Where do you get the funding, and how do you compensate your staff?" Chris asked as she realized the magnitude of this undertaking.

"My suggestion is to start small and grow from there. Volunteerism is crucial. We use church members from all denominations. In addition, volunteers from throughout the community are vital. An important part of our success comes from the clients volunteering themselves. Sometimes we have to 'volunteer them'. They need to feel a part of the community and feel valued. As they prove themselves, we give them increased responsibility, something most have never had. This is a good way for them to learn the skills required when they leave the shelter and try to rebuild their lives independently. I must tell you, however, that all do not make it. Sometimes, tough love is required, and we must ask people to leave our facility. If they do not follow our rules and try to improve their lives, we must make room for someone who will. It's sad but necessary."

"How about the money?" asked Becky.

The vast majority of the money comes from donations, so you'll have to recruit people to pound the pavement, getting local businesses, churches, and individuals to donate in the spirit of community. This is no small task. You also are fortunate that Justin is on board with you. He may find some city funds and apply for available grants if people only apply. I'll be happy to share specific organizations that focus on these types of projects with him."

What else sets your organization apart from so many that have failed?" inquired Chris.

"I don't know how true this is, but people have told me that my compassionate leadership, commitment to serving the marginalized, and insistence that we follow a vision of social change inspires others to get involved. We get donations from all over the country now because they know our formula is working, at least working at a higher rate than most."

"You mentioned social justice. What do you mean by that?"

"All God's Children works tirelessly every day to address systematic issues that contributed to homelessness., such as poverty, inequality, and a lack of affordable housing. We advocate for policy changes and strive to raise awareness about homelessness as a social issue. I can't tell you how many times I've been arrested while protesting one issue or another. We need a higher minimum wage, we need available and affordable healthcare, we need free job training, we need transportation opportunities for folks to get to and from work, and we need childcare facilities that nurture and teach the children, not just a warehouse for them to languish every day. The needs are tremendous. And Becky, Justin told me your husband is a U.S. Congressman in your area. He can be a champion in addressing these social issues from his seat in Washington."

"I'd like to think so, Ed, but I have some work to do with him first to get him on board. He's a compassionate man, so I hope we will eventually see eye to eye on this issue."

"We're taking too much of your time, Ed," Chris said as a transition to ending the meeting. What have we missed that you think we should know?"

"Ladies, the biggest part of this is the spiritual side. You, your staff, and your clients all have to believe in the power of God Almighty. Everything that you do must revolve around His will, not yours. You'll be fine if you keep

God at the center of everything you do. Instill the love of God in everyone that interacts with your shelter."

"Amen," Chris responded. "Amen. Thank you, Ed, for your insights. This has been extremely helpful and, I must say, overwhelming. But we're committed to making a difference, so we'll take one step at a time and celebrate our minor victories along the way. Thank you again."

"My pleasure, and feel free to call me again. I'd love for you to spend a day in Philadelphia with me, and I'll show you our facility and introduce you to our staff. Good luck, and may God bless you."

"God bless you," responded the two women simultaneously.

Becky and Chris looked at each other after the screen went blank, each with a look of "What in the world are we doing? Can we do this?"

Chris broke the trance and said to Becky, "Let's go home and pray about this and pray about what we heard from Ed and talk again in a few days."

"Good idea. This will take much prayer."

Oakdale United Methodist Church

Sunday

10:35 am

Christina continued to look up from her spot behind the piano, hoping to see Jasmine and Mia sleek through the front doors, but they were nowhere to be seen through the announcements or the first hymn. During the refrain of the second hymn, however, they eased in and found seats in the corner where no one was nearby. Christina smiled at them and continued playing. The service went as always: prayers, Joys and Concerns, Apostles Creed, Offering, scripture read, followed by Pastor Don taking his spot behind the gorgeous wooden pulpit. This week's sermon, similar to all that he delivered, revolved around discipleship and spiritual growth. About a third of the way through his sermon, as he rambled from one subject to another and his voice went from a whisper to a shout, something happened. Pastor Don grabbed his chest, perspiration poured from his forehead, dizziness overcame his sense of balance, and he stumbled off to the side of the pulpit. He reached for anything to prevent him from falling and grabbed the flagpole flying the American flag. He tried to stay upright but to no avail. As vomit spewed from his mouth, he landed flat on his face with a mighty thud. A collective gasp filled the sanctuary as three or four people seated up front rushed to his side. None knew what to do and only gently shook him and repeated, "Pastor Don, are you okay?"

Life Goes On

He was not okay, and fear paralyzed the shocked congregation, rendering them incapable of offering any real help. From the back corner raced a biracial homeless woman dressed in an old, tattered cotton dress, pushed the do-gooders to the side and pointed at one man in the front pew (the hearing aid row), and demanded, "Call 911."

She evaluated the situation quickly. Since there was no response to the shaking, she rolled him onto his back, tilted his head slightly, and tilted his chin to open the airway. She placed her ear near the pastor's mouth and nose, looking for signs of breathing. His chest was not rising and falling, and she heard no breathing sounds. She saw or heard nothing, no signs of life. Immediately, she straddled the lifeless hypocrite, placed the heel of one hand on the center of his chest, put her other hand on top, and interlocked her fingers. With her shoulders directly over his chest, she locked her elbows and used her upper body weight to press straight down on his chest. She pressed down about two inches and compressed the chest at a rate of over 100 compressions per minute, letting the chest rise back up between compressions. The congregation remained stunned and useless.

From nowhere, Mia, the homeless 8-9-year-old girl whom everyone in the congregation shunned, stood in front of them all and began singing without prompting.

Amazing grace, how sweet the sound

That saved a wretch like me

Jeff Jenkins

I once was lost, but now I'm found

Was blind, but now I see

'Twas grace that taught my heart to fear

And grace my fears relieved

How precious did this grace appear

The hour I first believed

Through many dangers, toils and snares

We have already come

'Twas grace has brought us safe thus far

And grace will lead us home.

When we've been here ten thousand years

Bright, shining as the sun

We've no less days to sing God's praise

Then when we've first begun

Amazing grace, how sweet the sound

That saved a wretch like me.

Her soothing voice resonated throughout the sound-friendly sanctuary. Slowly, a couple of other people grabbed hymnals and joined Mia, singing, then ten or more, and soon the entire congregation sang as Jasmine continued her work on the pastor. After thirty chest compressions, Jasmine administered two rescue breaths by keeping Don's head and chin tilted, pinched his nose closed, covered his mouth with hers, and breathed air into his listless body until his chest rose. Each breath lasted about one second. Then, back to the next thirty compressions.

Jasmine hollered to the singing, stunned United Methodists, "Do you have an AED?"

A quick "No" came from a gentleman close to the pulpit. Jasmine continued the compressions, followed by two rescue breaths, praying that the EMS personnel would arrive soon. She was exhausted but never slowed down the rate of compressions, always staying well above one hundred per minute. Mia kept singing as a hysterical Becky remained praying by her husband's side.

What seemed like thirty minutes was actually closer to six when three EMS personnel rushed through the church's front doors with a backpack full of equipment and a stretcher in hand. One immediately took over the CPR from a relieved Jasmine. Another one checked for a pulse and announced, "I feel a weak pulse." The third asked questions about Pastor Don's medical history, particularly cardiac episodes, of which there was none to Becky's knowledge. While asking questions, an EMS professional applied an oxygen mask over the patient's face.

While the CPR continued, the third medical professional turned on the AED that they brought, attached the electrode pads to Don's chest, and followed the prompts provided by the AED.

The machine quickly analyzed the situation and recommended a shock. The rescuers, following the prompt, stood clear, and a shock struck Don's chest, causing a mild bounce. A rescuer rechecked his pulse and ascertained that it had a regular rhythm and appeared stronger than when they first arrived. One continued with CPR as the other two prepared the stretcher to rush Don to the hospital.

John and Joane Brewbaker grabbed Becky's arm when the stretcher left the church, put her in the back of their SUV, and, with lights blinking, followed the rescue squad to the hospital.

The singing stopped when Don left the church on a stretcher, but the praying continued. The Lay Leader, Charles Humphries, stood up and said a prayer as the others bowed their heads. Then, another church member stood and prayed a heartfelt prayer, and another and another in a popcorn-style prayer service. When the prayers stopped, they silently prayed before Mr. Humphries said, "Amen."

The shell-shocked congregation filed out of the church without the usual chatter but with their heads bowed in a respectful formation. Mia and her mom, Jasmine, stayed until all were gone, kneeled at the altar, and silently prayed. As they stood to leave, Mia noticed that the collection plates were full of money and that the doors were wide open, with no one in sight. Jasmine picked up both plates, walked through the hall out of the sanctuary toward the church offices, found the pastor's office, and placed the plates on his desk. They locked the back door, found their way back through the sanctuary, locked the front doors from the inside, and silently walked back to the overpass.

Oakdale Community Hospital

Oakdale, NC

Monday

1:55 pm

Rick's long-time friend and pastor, Don Thornton, lay in a hospital room in a medically induced coma. The hospital staff only allowed one visitor at a time, so when a church member/friend walked out, Becky nodded to Rick to go into the room. The sight of his friend lying unconscious in the bed yesterday, with a ventilator crammed down his throat, is one that Rick could not unsee. Rick reached out and gently held his confidant's cold, clammy hand, talking to him with no response. But Rick talked. Rick told his friend about the one-night affair, including the details of Alek's worldly beauty, smell, intrigue, and trap this beautiful devil dog set for him. Sharing with his friend, he recounted the story of the envelopes that followed and how his incorrect vote resulted in the abduction of his innocent son, Ethan. He confessed that his son, although making progress, still had a long way to go to return to a fun-loving, adventurous young boy. He cried while holding Don's hand as he lamented that he ruined his son's childhood just because of a stupid mistake that he had made. He confided with his comatose friend that his marriage was a façade because of him. Instead of spending time with his wife, he prioritized his wealthy donors. Sometimes, he knew more about what the donor's kids were doing than he did about his own flesh and blood children. He told Don about Cheryl's dramatic resignation and that the most penetrating point she made happened when she returned to the office after storming out. She looked the congressperson in the eyes, telling him that he was a terrible dad. Could it be obvious to everyone? Rick cried, held the cold, lifeless hand of his friend, and cried. He cried like never before. This was the worst moment of his life. Then he held the hand tighter and prayed. He prayed for his friend to recover, but he also prayed for himself. He prayed that the Lord would free him from the misery that he found himself and would give him peace. And he prayed for forgiveness for what he had done to his family. Rick cleaned up his wet eyes, blew his nose, reclaimed his composure, and the desolate shell of a man shuffled out of the cold, white hospital room. He met Chris in the lobby, hugged her, and cried into her ear, "I'm sorry."

She, of course, took it to mean that he was sorry for her husband's heart attack, and for his unlikely recovery. Yes, he meant just that, but she did not realize that he was also sorry for his pitiful life of deceit and power-hungry ways. Maybe he was admitting that he was indeed a sorry man.

Cannon House Office Building

Washington, DC

Tuesday 6:15 am

After driving back to Washington after his emotional visit with a non-responsive friend and pastor, Rick sat in his office by himself, with no staff expected for over an hour. He needed to think. Before and after hours, his office offered a quiet place to reflect and ponder. His anxiety heightened upon returning from the press conference at AKE, where he spoke eloquently in favor of the company for establishing new wetlands. He knew it was all horse feathers and that he had become a huge hypocrite for talking the talk yet voting according to the way Ralph at AKE dictated. Money talks in politics. The enormous elephant in the lonely room was the Evil One. He knew for a fact, with no evidence, that the Evil One was indeed a Russian agent. He didn't know how high up the chain the Russian plot went, and he didn't know how many other U.S. politicians were also being extorted, but he knew he was in way over his country doctor head.

What he had done to his loyal and capable staff member, Cheryl, stung. He wanted to tell her the truth, but he knew that was not an option. While he deserved the tongue-lashing she put on him, it didn't ease the pain of hearing it. He had let down his wide-eyed, idealistic staffer. She left the building, her job, and probably activism, forever. He couldn't get out of his mind the last words that she said to him, "And you're a sorry father, too."

The Speaker of the House visited Rick shortly after he voted to disallow any money aid to the country's NATO allies. He blew out the trapped congressman worse than either parent or any teacher ever had, maybe as bad as Cheryl's beat-down just a few days ago. In reality, he had never given anyone a reason to be so mad at him his entire life. He had been the "Golden Boy," always doing the right thing. "What has happened to me?" he thought. "Who am I."

Rick reflected on his life; a good-looking, intelligent high school athlete. He excelled at the medical school of the major university in the state, did his residency at Johns Hopkins, and returned home to serve the community where he grew up. He married his high school sweetheart, Becky, and has three precocious and loving young boys. Yet, he all but abandoned them upon entering politics. He loved the attention of being a U.S. Congressman. The power that he exerted fueled his innermost desire to be the star again as he was in high school. Money rolled in as soon as big donors with their own agendas learned that he could be bought. But where did the power and money get him? He was in a mess, and he saw no way out.

"I can't tell Becky of my fling," he thought. "I can't risk the lives of my children or my wife by standing up to the world's biggest bully, Russia. I can't."

Morose to the bone, Rick felt enormous guilt for the affair, for accepting bribes, for voting against his conscience, for letting down his party, and for betraying the trust of his constituents. This, coupled with the woefulness of seeing his friend, his pastor, lying in bed cold and listless, was too much to bear.

In his dismal state, Rick reached into his desk drawer, pulled out a clean sheet of letterhead, and with his antique fountain pen given to him by his grandfather, the very one his grandfather used during his career as a country doctor to write prescriptions. Rick used it in Washington to sign official documents, bills, and the like. He dipped the historical pen into an ink well on his desk and wrote.

My Dearest Beck,

I am so disconsolate over my actions these past few years. I abandoned you and the children, have been a terrible husband, and now I find myself letting down the very people who I came to Washington to serve. I let the glitz, particularly the power and money of this dreadful city, take over my brain and my Christian upbringing. I don't know why you stayed with me through this, but I am grateful that you did.

I have put you and the boys in danger by my actions, and I cannot bear the thought of anything happening to any of you because of my indiscretions.

Know that I love you, and I wish there were another answer to my predicament, but there is none.

With all my love,

Rick

PS The enclosed sheet has account numbers and instructions on accessing money that I have offshore.

Rick folded the handwritten letter, stuck it in an envelope, licked and sealed it, and placed it in the center of his desk addressed to "Becky—Personal."

Next, he methodically retrieved all the correspondence from the Evil One and put it into a small portable Office Depot file folder. With another pen, he wrote the story of Alek, the pictures, the abduction of his son, the voting demands, everything. These notes also went into the cheap file folder. With heavy shipping tape, Rick wrapped the folder closed and, with a magic marker, wrote in large bold print, "FBI." He left this beside his letter to Becky.

With no other option left for this forlorn shell of a man that once was, Rick unlocked the bottom drawer of his desk, reached to the back, and retrieved a loaded Glock 19. He bought the compact and easy-to-use handgun after January 6th, when the helpless doctor ran for safety with other members of Congress. The sales associate explained that it was a 9mm, a popular caliber for self-defense because of its manageable recoil and effectiveness.

Oakdale Community Hospital

Oakdale, NC

Tuesday 8:55 am

Downcast and full of trepidation, Christina met the cardiologist as he made his rounds. The doctor once again explained that he and the hospital team chose to put Don into a medically induced coma because of Cardiogenic Shock, which, in plain language, means that the heart cannot pump enough blood to meet the body's needs. This sometimes occurs with severe heart attack victims. This medical procedure reduces the heart's oxygen demand and allows it to recover. The team also believed that a medically induced coma could protect the brain from further injury while they addressed the underlying cardiac issues. The medical professionals did not know how long Jasmine had performed CPR, nor did they know how effective she was in her efforts. Thus, they took the conservative approach and induced the coma.

The doctor informed Christina that her husband was doing well. His breathing remained strong after they removed the ventilator, and his heart rate was steady, although still a little weak. His oxygen levels had improved. So now, the consensus among the medical colleagues was to bring the pastor out of the coma. They explained that they would monitor him closely and put him back under if necessary. They wanted to start the procedure now.

Chris agreed as if she knew the alternatives; in this situation, she simply trusted the doctor.

She sat patiently by Don's side as the nurses gradually reduced the coma-inducing medications. Her thoughts bounced off of the walls. "What if there is brain damage?" she thought. "What if he lives but is a vegetable?" She cried and prayed as the 'waking up' process continued. Don showed signs of consciousness, opening his eyes just a tad. He responded ever so slightly to stimuli. Two hours passed. Four hours, now into the eighth, he opened his eyes fully, saw Chris, and smiled. Overcome with joy and gratitude, she hugged her awakening soulmate. A kind nurse lovingly but firmly pulled her away from Don as he continued to check his vitals. So far, so good. His heartbeat at fifty-five beats per minute, he breathed on his own, and he understood what Chris and others said in the room. If there was any brain damage, it appeared to be minimal, at least so far.

After another hour of 'weaning off' of the coma-inducing drugs, the head cardiologist reentered the stark ICU room to find an exhausted but jubilant Christina and a weak but functioning and talking patient. The doctor looked at both Don and Chris and said, "We have experienced a miracle here today. Thank God to the lady in your congregation who applied CPR so quickly and tirelessly. There is no doubt that she saved your life."

A confused Don asked Chris in a low, weak voice, "Who gave me CPR?"

"It was the homeless lady, Don. It was Jasmine, the homeless lady."

Tears once again flowed from Chris, and now, this time, tears filled Pastor Don Thornton's eyes as well.

Men's Restroom

Cannon House Office Building

Washington, DC

Tuesday

7:20 am

Rick did not yet know that on the very day that he escaped from the hell in which he now lived, the only option that made any sense to him was the same day that his cohort in a medically induced coma would 'wake up' with strong vitals, and appear to have avoided any debilitating brain damage, in a fashion that his cardiologist called a miracle. Rick was not so lucky. No miracle could save him now. He stashed the Glock in the inside pocket of his suit coat, left the office, and stared down a vacant hall. He eased into the bathroom, ensured that no one was in it, opened and entered a stall, closed and locked it. After lowering the seat lid, he sat down, hands shaking, trying desperately to think of another way out. There was none.

He had to do this. His guilt took over what little brain cells continued to operate in his sad state. So, he reached into his pocket, pulled out the Glock, and checked that it was fully loaded as if he anticipated needing more than one shot while switching off the safety. He raised the barrel of the gun an inch into his mouth, wrapped his lips around the cold steel barrel, tightened his grip on the trigger, and prayed one last prayer. "Lord, forgive me." He squeezed the trigger.

Oakdale Community Hospital

Oakdale, NC

Thursday 10:20 am

Pastor Don continued to make progress until he left the ICU, and the medical staff transferred him to a standard room within the Heart Center. Christina stayed at the hospital with him from 8:00 am to 9:00 pm. She went home at night, hoping to get a good night's sleep, a shower, and a change of clothes. The doctors believed that he would go home in a few days but with close supervision and a monitor. Church members were not allowed to visit, with rare exceptions, such as giving Chris a break to go to the cafeteria or at least walk around the courtyard outside.

Don's vitals remain strong, and the crew of doctors, P.A.s, and nurses all say that it is nothing short of a miracle that the pastor is still alive and that he suffered no apparent long-term brain damage. He's still fatigued, sleeps most of the day, and his mind is not one hundred percent sharp, but it's getting better every day.

A P.A. assigned to Pastor Thornton advised that they would refer him to the Cardiac Rehabilitation unit for supervised exercise training, education on heart-healthy lifestyle habits, and emotional support. She also explained that he will be on new medications to manage blood pressure, cholesterol levels, blood thinning, and heart function. She suggested fundamental lifestyle changes and emphasized the importance of adhering to them. He must lose weight, eat a heart-healthy diet, and stick to a regular exercise program. Pastor Don lay in bed listening, but he didn't like missing Sunday lunches at The Café or a church member's house. But he knew that he had to.

She asked about his stress levels at the church, and Don admitted that being a pastor was indeed stressful, and it sometimes brought him to a state of mild-to-moderate depression. She gave him ideas on how to mitigate stress. Dealing with the death of his long-time friend didn't help, which led the P.A. to suggest he join a support group and possibly counseling. He thought about the irony of this. He usually was the counselor, but now he needed counseling himself. She suggested that he take off at least a month from his regular church duties and keep visitors to a minimum, particularly those bringing casseroles and desserts. Although Don did not remember everything that was said between Chris and him and the written materials they received, he felt comfortable that he could get on the right track.

He was determined to do so, particularly since the experience that he had during the period from when he passed out at church until he woke up from the coma. Now that he was thinking clearly and could articulate his thoughts, his top priority was to tell Chris about the experience.

Oakdale United Methodist Church

Oakdale, NC

Sunday

10:30 am

The Reverend Al Baker, the District Superintendent for Oakdale's area, presided at the Sunday service, filling in for the recuperating pastor Don. During the welcome and announcements part of the service, Pastor Al stated the obvious: the church, and indeed the country, were shocked by the horrific loss of their friend, church member, doctor, and congressman, Rick Davis. He reminded everyone that Dr. The Reverend Charles Morton will preside over Davis's funeral, scheduled for that afternoon at the Oakdale Community Center. Reverend Morton, also a U.S. congressman, developed a close kinship with Rick over the past two years when they worked together in the House.

Pastor Al also updated the congregation on Pastor Don's condition, relaying that he was out of the ICU, in a regular room, and doing miraculously well. However, he still had a way to go with rehab and lifestyle changes, including a heart-healthy diet and reducing the stress in his life.

He then shared with the congregation what numerous doctors had told him during that scary time in the hospital, that if it were not for the heroic, quick action taken by Jasmine, Pastor Don would undoubtedly have died. Her take-charge approach to instructing a particular person to call 911, her tireless efforts administering CPR, and her knowledge to give two rescue breaths after every thirty compressions is why he is alive today and with no apparent brain damage. Immediately, the same congregation that shunned Jasmine and her daughter every Sunday that they attended the church, the same congregation that complained about how the two dressed, the same congregation that held their noses when in close vicinity of the two homeless souls, stood and applauded Jasmine. Tears filled her eyes as this unexpected adulation filled the room. Her face flushed with embarrassment. She looked at the floor to avoid eye contact, yet a shy smile filled her face. She raised her head, nodded to the grateful people, and mouthed, "Thank you. Thank you."

Vivian Woodruff, wife of Clyde Woodruff, a long-time large donor to the church, stood after the applause waned. The congregation had returned to their seated positions and announced, "And we are so grateful for

Jasmine's daughter, Mia, an eight-year-old who had the presence of mind to stand in front of these strangers and lead us in singing *Amazing Grace*. Her voice is phenomenal, far beyond her years, and it helped us all to focus on praying for our pastor when none of us knew what to do."

The congregation stood again, without prompting, and gave Mia a rousing standing ovation. Like her mom, Mia had expected no kudos and felt embarrassed, but she appreciated every second of the gratitude she received. Maybe for the first time in her brief life, Mia felt appreciated.

The service progressed along its typical sequence until the sermon. Pastor Al challenged the congregation to step up and take on a more prominent role in the tasks that Pastor Don had traditionally taken. He talked about how the laity of churches everywhere had somehow become lackadaisical, that they expected the minister to manage the church business, to visit the sick, to seek and help the needy, to teach Bible studies, to encourage others to visit the church, to preach inspirational sermons weekly, and to "Make disciples of Jesus Christ for the Transformation of the World," which is the mission of the United Methodist church. The laity seemed to think that their role was to attend church, to be fed, and to make monetary donations. He used Matthew 5:16 (NIV) to support his challenge, *"In the same way, let your light shine before others, that they may see your good deeds and glorify your Father in heaven."* He challenged the believers to show their faith through good deeds and positive actions so that others may witness the goodness of God.

Pastor Al continued his call for the laity to step up with another Bible verse, James 2:17 (NIV), *"In the same way, faith by itself, if not accompanied by action, is dead."* James emphasized the importance of professing faith and demonstrating it through actions. Faith should manifest in tangible deeds and efforts to serve others and uphold the teachings of Christ.

The last verse that the D.S. used to drive home his point came from 1 Peter 4:10 (NIV), *"Each of you should use whatever gift you have received to serve others, as faithful stewards of God's grace in its various forms."* This verse highlights the concept of stewardship and encourages believers to use their unique gifts and talents to serve others, thereby actively contributing to spreading God's grace and love in the world.

The service ended with an enthusiastic, motivated congregation slowly exiting the church, shaking hands with the D.S. and thanking him for such a motivational sermon. He asked that Jasmine and Mia stand in the vestibule with him as the Methodists left so that each could personally thank this unlikely duo. And they did, with love and appreciation. The parishioners made their way to their cars, knowing that changes were in store for the church. They knew that changes were necessary. They did not yet know, however, how remarkable and far-reaching the change would be.

Since Mia and Jasmine were with the D.S. greeting the grateful churchgoers as they left the church, Christina spoke to them before they inconspicuously slipped out, as has been their habit. Chris reached out for Jasmine's hand, looked her in the eyes, and with conviction and compassion, told the two, "Jasmine, here's what I want you to do, and I'm not taking no for an answer. Go to the overpass, pack up your tent and belongings, and meet me on the side of the road beside the encampment. You're going to come live with Don and me until you can get on your feet."

"No, Mrs. Thornton, we can't do that." That's too much to ask of you."

"Nonsense. You saved my husband's life. And I need your help. He's coming home this week, we pray, and I need your help to take care of him and to keep the house going. This is not charity; you'll be working for your keep."

"I don't know. I don't want to impose."
"You're not imposing. You are helping me when I need it most."

"What does Mr. Thornton think about this? He never seemed to welcome us, and I thought he did not want us to even be at the church. Now we're going to live in his home. I just don't think that it'll work."

"Oh, it'll work. Trust me, it will work. Don't you worry about him; I'll deal with him. You just pack up your gear and meet me beside the encampment. I'll pick you up at 1:00 pm. That will give me time to be at the 4:00 pm funeral. And don't say 'no' again."

"Yes, ma'am. Thank you. We'll be there at 1:00.

Oakdale Community Hospital

Oakdale, NC

Sunday 2:20 pm

After a light lunch of lettuce, cottage cheese, and chicken salad, Chris headed to the hospital to visit with Don, check with the medical staff about his progress, and inform him that two homeless females would live in his house when he returned home. Although she talked big to Jasmine, she didn't know how to approach this subject with her self-centered husband. She knew it was the right thing to do, and she did need help around the house while he recuperated, but she still was concerned that this news may send him over the top. She proceeded to the hospital full of faith the Lord would give her the words to use in telling Don and that the Lord would open Don's heart, even his damaged heart, to the idea.

Upon entering his hospital room, she saw a man who had made progress. His color had returned, and he sat up in the bed with wires and tubes attached to his arms and chest, with a monitor overhead blinking, chirping, with lines representing his heartbeat scrolling across the screen. Before she could even speak to a nurse, she asked him how he felt, told him about the service in which the D.S. presided, or even explained to him that she invited two homeless people to live with them at the parsonage. He started talking. "Chris, I have to get out of here to attend Rick's funeral. Talk to the doctor for me, please."

"I know, Don, but you cannot go. We don't need another funeral right now. You are not yet strong enough, and to be away from this hospital bed and the care you're receiving would be flat-out dangerous. I'm sorry. I know you want to go."

"I know Chris. I'm still in shock and want to begin the healing process. There's just too much for me to handle right now, particularly with what I have to tell you."

"Don, we will stream the funeral worldwide via Zoom." I'll ask one of the nurses to help you set up the computer so you can at least view the service."

"Okay, please do."

He was busting at the seams to tell Chris about the near-death experience that he had. With no one else in the room, the story was coming out. And it was coming out NOW.

"Chris, you will not believe what happened to me. I'm not sure when it happened; it may have been in the church when I fell out, it may have been while that lady performed CPR on me, maybe it happened on the way to the hospital, or possibly while I was in the medically induced coma, but it happened."

"What happened?"

"It was just like what Saul described in Acts on the road to Damascus. I saw Jesus face to face. I talked to Jesus. He was here just as much as you are here yourself."

"What did he say?"

"Chris, it was amazing. A bright light from heaven flashed around me, and I fell to the ground. I heard His voice say, 'Don, Don, why are you persecuting me?'

I replied, 'Who are you, Lord?'

The voice replied, 'I am Jesus, whom you are prosecuting.'"

"Are you sure you were just not revisiting a sermon that you have given countless times?"

"No, this was real. No, this was real. I became blinded, and a woman approached me and laid her hands on me. She said, 'Brother Don, the Lord Jesus, who appeared to you on your way here, has sent me to help you regain your sight and be filled with the Holy Spirit.' Immediately, I felt something like scales falling from my eyes, and I regained my sight. Chris, Jesus himself asked me what I had done for the 'least of these.' I had nothing. I've talked the talk, but really, I have done nothing."

"I've read about near-death experiences Don. Some scientists believe that they occur in some people because of biological processes in the brain, particularly in times of extreme stress or decreased oxygen supply. Do you think that it was simply a chemical issue in your brain?"

"No, I'm certain. I talked to Jesus Himself, and it was not pleasant. He scolded me for not inviting Him in when He was a stranger. He said that I did not clothe Him when He needed clothes. He added that when He was sick, I did not help Him. When I asked Him when all this happened, it was like He quoted directly from Matthew 25. He looked me in the eyes and told me in no uncertain terms, 'Truly I tell you, whatever you did not do for one of the least of these, you did not do for me.' Chris, it was terrifying. He told me that He would come again and separate people into two groups, like separating sheep from goats. The Father blesses one group and will receive their inheritance, and the Kingdom is prepared for them. A curse awaits the other group, and they will enter the eternal fire prepared for the devil and his angels. Chris, I've preached this sermon repeatedly, but this time it is real. Jesus told me that I was in the wrong group, but through His grace, I had another chance to join the righteous group. I know you think I'm crazy, but it was real. It was real!"

"I believe you, honey; I believe you. Close your eyes, relax, and get some rest. We can talk about this some more later."

"Okay, but I'm telling you, Jesus talked to me directly."

As soon as Don's eyes closed, Chris bolted to the recliner in the hospital room, fired up her iPad, and looked up "Near-Death Experiences" or, as she quickly learned, NDEs. She wanted to see if there was a logical explanation for what Don believes was a talk with Jesus, face to face. She first discovered that what she had read and told Don was indeed an explanation that some proposed. Neurobiological processes occurring in the brain during times of extreme stress or a decreased oxygen supply may lead to alterations in consciousness and perceptions, which are characteristics of NDEs. The key word that she noticed was "may." The scientists are speculating.

In addition, there are psychological explanations such as beliefs, expectations, and cultural influences that may play a role in shaping an individual's experience during near-death situations. Again, "may".

Another website suggested that studies have found that the content and interpretation of NDEs can vary across different cultural and religious contexts. This suggests that cultural factors may influence the phenomenology of NDEs. Chris struggled with this explanation but noted once again the word becoming an enormous elephant in the research; "may."

Some researchers view NDEs as an altered state of consciousness that may occur spontaneously or in response to specific physiological conditions. Altered states of consciousness, such as meditation, psychedelic experiences, or dissociative states, may share similarities with NDEs in terms of subjective experiences. "May".

While scientific research has provided valuable insights into the psychological and neurobiological mechanisms underlying NDEs, the subjective nature of these experiences makes them difficult to fully explain or understand within a purely scientific framework.

With all of her reading and research, while Don peacefully slept, Chris found no definitive answer to what Don said was a talk with Jesus. Maybe he did hear directly from Jesus. Who was she to dispute it? One thing was obvious from her reading: Many people in the days and weeks following the NDE may engage in introspection and reflection as they try to make sense of what happened. Some individuals feel profoundly changed by their NDE, leading to shifts in beliefs, priorities, and outlook on life. Although Chris could not yet be sure, she became more and more convinced that this was happening with Don. Time will tell, but for now, she too believed that Jesus talked to Don, telling him that he was currently in the unrighteous group and that he had better change and change quickly, or he would stay in the wrong group on judgment day. She was so engrossed in the research that time ran faster than she did, causing a minor panic when she realized it was 3:45 pm and the funeral started in fifteen minutes. She bolted out of the room, reminded the nurse to wake Don and help him view the service, and off she bolted to the jam-packed community center.

Oakdale Community Center

Sunday

4:00 pm

Reverend Charles Morton, a retired Presbyterian minister and current member of the U.S. Congress representing a district in upstate South Carolina, presided at the service. As everyone expected, the Community Center was filled with those perceptive enough to arrive at least an hour early, occupying every seat. After all the seats and the standing room around the perimeter were taken, mourners continued to arrive. The organizers directed these folks to the gymnasium next door, where they set up a big screen to view the service remotely. Many dignitaries from Washington arrived, and the organizers immediately directed them to the ten rows they had reserved. Included in that group was the Speaker of the House and the Vice-President of the United States, who had flown in on Air Force II to the Cherry Point Air Station. She traveled via motorcade for forty minutes from Cherry Point to Oakdale. She arrived at the community center surrounded by gobs of Secret Service personnel.

Congressman Davis's wife, three small boys, his parents, and other close family members congregated in a room adjacent to the expansive main hall, crying, consoling each other, and waiting for 4:00 pm. Reverend Morton gathered the family in a circle where they joined hands, one with another, and he prayed. After the "Amen" a funeral home staff member led the family into the hall and raised his hands to indicate to the congregation to stand. The family stood together in their designated seats at the front, opposite the dignitaries.

Pastor Charles took over.

"Jesus said, I am the resurrection, and I am the life.

Those who believe in me, even though they die, yet shall they live,

And whoever lives and believes in me shall never die.

I am the Alpha and the Omega, the beginning and the end, the first and the last.

I died, and behold I am alive forevermore,

And I hold the keys of hell and death.

Because I live, you shall live also."

He continued with the Greeting,

"Friends, we have gathered here to praise God

And to witness to our faith as we celebrate the life of Frederick John Davis.

We come together in grief, acknowledging our human loss.

May God grant us grace; that pain, we may find comfort; in sorrow, hope; in death, resurrection."

After a prayer, a song sung by the church choir, reading the 23rd Psalm, and reading three scripture passages, Reverend Morton began the eulogy.

> *"Today, we gather with heavy hearts to mourn the loss of our dear colleague, friend, husband, son, and father. This is a profound and tragic loss for us all, including this supporting community, the state, and the country."*

The oratory skills honed by years of preaching and, more recently, serving as a congressman shone through. He had every ear perked up, absorbing every word as he continued.

> *"He dedicated his life to helping others, first as a doctor and later serving you fine folks in public service. He worked tirelessly advocating for the needs and rights of his constituents. His commitment to justice and equality was evident in every piece of legislation that he championed. He was a man of immense integrity, compassion, and courage. His kindness, empathy, and dedication touched the lives of everyone he knew and those in which he served."*

Although Becky was full of joy hearing the polished preacher continuing about this great man, she couldn't help but wonder if this was the same man that all but deserted his family, and after reading the letter written by her husband just minutes before he pulled the trigger on himself. She focused again on the preacher's words when he talked about his impact and legacy.

> *His work will leave a lasting impact for generations to come as he fought to improve our society. He leaves a legacy of tireless advocacy and unwavering dedication to public service."*

Some of his colleagues silently and inconspicuously elbowed their colleagues beside them, also thinking that the minister must be talking about someone other than Dr. Davis.

Paster Charles addressed the obvious, the waste, and the unnecessary way in which the congressman died.

> *"My friend Don faced many battles, both public and private, and today, we acknowledge the importance of mental health. We must remember that even those who appear strong can be fighting unseen struggles."*

Congressman Morton pledged to use this senseless death as an impetus for the United States Congress to tackle the epidemic of mental health that is eating away at this country from the inside out. Other members of Congress in attendance aggressively nodded approval, knowing that this would not go further than the Oakdale Community Center Hall.

Congressman Morton continued for a solid forty-five minutes. When would he ever get the chance to speak in front of so many colleagues and, most importantly, the Vice-President? He closed with a pat four-or five-minute sermon, inviting all that hear his voice in the hall and through Zoom, to find peace and comfort in Jesus Christ. He encouraged them to repent, to curl up in the loving arms of Jesus, and to know that God is with them, now, here, always.

> *"Rest in peace, dear friend. Your work and your spirit will live on in our memories. Though Fredrick John Davis is no longer with us, his light continues to shine and to guide us. Amen."*

After a brief silent prayer, Pastor Charles closed the service with a prayer, followed by another hymn by the church choir, and a Committal Prayer spoken from the floor while placing one hand on the urn holding Rick's ashes. After everyone prayed the Lord's Prayer, Pastor Charles led the congregation out of the building directed by the professional staff from the local funeral home.

Politicians, being politicians, gathered outside the Community center and shook hands, spoke among themselves, and inquired about the candidates seeking to fill his seat. Everyone, including the vice president, sought Becky, hugged, and offered their thoughts and prayers. As quickly as they arrived, they were gone.

Now, the hard part for Becky. How would she handle the realization that her husband, her high school sweetheart, her provider, was gone, really gone?

An inconspicuous lady, dressed in conservative southern-looking church clothes with her hair pulled back and only light makeup, sat near the back during the service. The locals assumed she was a Washington staffer. The Washington contingent thought she was a local. No one thought anything about her. And Aleksandre Wojic, or whatever her name was, vanished out of sight.

Cannon House Office Building

Washington, DC

Monday

9:10 am

Word spread like a California wildfire around the capital about Rick's death. Shock, disbelief, and deep sadness swept through the entire building. Rick's staff assembled in his office, crying uncontrollably, dazed, not having a clue what Rick had endured before that single shot from his Glock.

Speculation about who his successor might be spread rapidly almost as soon as the blood was mopped up in the bathroom. According to law, the Speaker of the House must officially notify the Governor of North Carolina of the vacancy. That was routine. The Governor is responsible for issuing a writ of election, an official order calling for a special election to fill the vacant seat. North Carolina law specifies the procedures for conducting special elections. He must set a date for the special primary and general election, and the timeline must allow enough time for candidates to file, for ballots to be prepared, and for a proper election to be conducted. The special election winner will be inaugurated as a member of the U.S. House of Representatives and will fulfill the rest of the term.

Although not happy with Rick and his erratic behavior of late, the Speaker was concerned about how this election may go. The newly elected congressman may be less loyal to him than was Dr. Davis. He currently holds a razor-thin majority, and if a candidate from the opposing party manages to win, it will severely shake his hopes of implementing his agenda. The fact that it would be several months without a congressman from Rick's district, thus no vote from that district, had the already nervous speaker on the verge of panicking. But time marches on, and he will overcome this bump in the road just as he has skirted previous political disasters. First, he must discern the potential candidates and work to get the right one elected. Even though his colleague, a hometown star athlete, a respected doctor, a father of three, and a husband is dead from suicide, a suicide brought on in no small part by his House is only an afterthought. He must hold on to the power that he had scratched and clawed for years to achieve. He sure as heck would not allow the actions of one distraught member to ruin his personal goals.

FBI Headquarters

J. Edgar Hoover Building

935 Pennsylvania Avenue

Washington, DC

Tuesday

8:15 pm

After receiving the package from Congressman Davis, the FBI prepared and activated a plan at once. This appeared to be direct interference, blackmail, and terrorism by the Russians with a United States Congressman. And the Bureau did not know how deep this plot went. Were there others under their influence? How about senators? Was it even feasible that the President himself was involved with a foreign adversary? Rick's package and written narrative of the events leading to his suicide was a big break for the FBI, and they jumped on it.

The FBI dispatched two agents to Oakdale to protect the deceased congressman's family. No one saw them or suspected anything out of the ordinary by their presence. They were invisible in plain sight.

Life Goes On

Parsonage

Oakdale UMC

Tuesday

9:15 pm

After a long hot shower at the church parsonage, Jasmine felt cleaner than she had in months, maybe longer. The guest room had shampoo, conditioner, and a fancy, sweet-smelling soap that Jasmine had never experienced. Mia also enjoyed a similar experience and went to bed, an actual bed with clean sheets and a fluffy pillow. She thought that she did not know what heaven was like, but it couldn't be much better than this. The exhausted eight-year-old fell into a deep, pleasant sleep only minutes after her head hit the pillow.

Jasmine knew that Mrs. Thornton had only eaten hospital food for the last several days and not much of it, so she searched the kitchen, determined to have some sort of home-cooked meal for the tired wife when she came home from visiting with her husband. She found a pork chop, some string beans, a tomato, some butter beans, and a couple of potatoes in the kitchen. When Christina dragged herself through the back door, she couldn't believe what Jasmine had prepared. She hugged the homeless heroine, cried, and thanked her immensely. She washed up, sat down, prayed, and dug it. It was delicious. She tried to share some with Jasmine but insisted she had already eaten.

Jasmine sat with her and listened as Christina shared the day's events.

They both heard the bed calling, so they said goodnight and went to their separate rooms. Christina cried again when she laid down, put her head on the pillow, and smelled the wonderful fragrance of the freshly washed sheets that Jasmine and Mia had washed. Jasmine is a godsend, she thought. Sleep overtook the physically and emotionally spent pastor's wife.

Oakdale Community Hospital

Oakdale, NC

Tuesday

10:05 pm

Don phased in and out of sleep the entire day. The medications relaxed him to the point of drowsiness, but when awake, his brain raced. "What to do about the disaffiliation vote? How will I inform the congregation that my priorities in life and with the church changed? Those who have grown accustomed to the nice do-nothing routine of the past were in for a rude awakening. Would they stay with the church? When I preach inclusion, reach out to the community (all parts of the community), and demand action to go along with prayer, what will their reaction be? I need to call Justin to tell him that I want to help the individuals in the homeless community. I need to talk to

John Brewbaker about calling a special meeting of the Administrative Council as soon as they let me out of here. Maybe I should start working on my sermon for my first Sunday back." Ideas continued to flow as he nodded back to sleep. The doctor's advice about slowing down, relaxing, and reducing stress had not kicked in. He was sprinting wide-open, lying in bed with tubes and wires attached to his arms and chest. He had to get it done.

Parsonage

Oakdale United Methodist Church

Wednesday

7:35 am

After a much-needed eight hours of sound sleep, Chris woke up to the scrumptious aroma of fried bacon. She found Jasmine cooking breakfast of scrambled eggs, bacon, grits, toast, and a fresh cup of coffee. Jasmine wore a blouse, pants, and sandals that Chris had given to her, and she looked rather lovely. With combed hair, a shower, and decent clothes, Jasmine's plain, wholesome beauty shined through. And with her smile, she was gorgeous. Mia ate cereal and orange juice before catching the bus to school. After a delicious breakfast that Jasmine and Chris enjoyed together, Chris cleaned the dishes prior to going to the hospital to see Don.

"No," insisted Jasmine. "You go to the hospital, and I'll clean up the dishes and the house. You go take care of your husband."

"Jasmine, you're terrific, thank you. When I get back, you, Mia, and I will go clothing shopping, and we can discuss how you may help me take care of Don when he comes home. In the meantime, here's one hundred dollars. Call a taxi and go grocery shopping for tonight and tomorrow."

"Oh, Mrs. Thornton, you are the kindest person I know."

"My name is Chris. And tonight, I want to talk to you about some plans I have been working on to help the homeless in the community. I need your help."

"God bless you, Chris."

After Chris scurried out, Jasmine held the one-hundred-dollar bill in her hand and looked at it, wondering how long it had been since she had seen that much money, if ever. She tucked the bill in her pants pocket, rolled up her sleeves, and started cleaning the dishes. She planned to have the house spotless, food cooked, and ready to talk to Chris about the needs of her friends at the overpass when she returned.

The Kremlin

Moscow, Russia

Wednesday

8:50 am (Russian Time)

Speaking in his native Russian language, Sergei Morozov, the prime Minister of the Russian Federation, told his assistant in a quiet voice so that no hidden microphones could pick up the sound, "I don't remember ever seeing the Boss so mad as he was the other day."

"What had him fired up?"

"I informed him that one of our assets in America, Aleksandre Wojic, went to the funeral of the Congressman who committed suicide.

The Prime Minister is the second-highest-ranking official in the Russian Federation. He is the head of government and runs the country's executive branch, overseeing the implementation of laws and managing the administration's daily operations. The President of Russia appoints the Prime Minister, and the State Duma (the lower house of the Federal Assembly of Russia) must also approve the appointment. In Russia, the approval by the State Duma is only a formality; the President micromanages everything, including hand-picking his top assistants. In reality, his assistants' principal duty is to agree with the President. The President deals with dissent swiftly and harshly.

The President for the last eighteen years, Kuri Kuznetsov, just about blew a gasket when he learned Alek had made such a stupid move. "Doesn't she know that she compromised our entire operation in the U.S. Congress?" he yelled at his long-time Prime Minister. "Doesn't she know that our hold on the Congress requires utmost secrecy? If she gets caught, which is highly likely, she could expose other assets we have in place, and the bumbling idiot congressmen that we control may be revealed. She is no longer an asset; she is now a huge liability. Send for her to come home now!"

Prime Minister Motozon gave the orders immediately and informed President Kuznetsov to expect her to be on Russian soil in two days.

Aleksandre Wojic boarded the Russian-made private jet, an Ilyushin Il-96, the same afternoon as she received her orders from the Prime Minister. The Russian Federation often uses this long-range, wide-body aircraft for intercontinental flights and government and VIP transport. The flight went smoothly, and Alek enjoyed a full-course Russian lunch, one like she could not find in the U.S. She started with a Borscht, a beet soup with cabbage, potatoes, and usually beef, served with a dollop of sour cream. She devoured the scrumptious main course of chicken Kiev served with a side of Kasha, a buckwheat porridge. Rye bread and black tea rounded out her meal. She found room for a Pirozhki, a small baked bun filled with sweet fillings, for dessert. She couldn't remember when she had such a fine Russian lunch. Alek nodded off after such a gourmet delight, only to awaken with violent abdominal cramps, a high fever, an excruciating headache, and extreme fatigue and weakness. The beautiful, smart, and outgoing Aleksandre Wojic died within an hour. There was no mention of her death in any Russian media, and no one in the U.S. even knew about her, so no obituary, no announcement in the Washington Post. Nothing. She just ceased to exist.

Cannon House Office Building

Washington, DC

Friday

11:15 pm

    Marcus Jones worked as a custodian in the Cannon Building for a little over three years. This was a second job for Mr. Jones in that he worked as an Uber driver during the day in Washington, DC. His wife worked a day job as a custodian in another government building. She fixed supper for the kids, bathed them, read them books at bedtime, and put them in their beds. Between the two, they made just enough to support themselves and their two small children. The strange man had not approached Mr. Jones outside the Cannon building for several days. He didn't ask questions; he just knew that one hundred dollars simply to put an envelope on a congressman's desk was easy and much needed. Jones realized that something was shady about this. Who paid that just to deliver an envelope? But he'd take it. He hoped he saw the hooded man again that night because the rent was due, but he did not. So, he went about emptying trash, vacuuming the carpeted floors, mopping the tile floors, dusting, and, as a bonus for the office personnel, spraying a sweet-smelling deodorizer throughout the offices.

Just as he had done for the last three years, he left at midnight and walked to the parking garage next to the Cannon Building. Out of nowhere, as he crossed from one side of the indoor parking lot to the other, a black SUV with no headlights barreled straight toward him, going well over sixty miles an hour in the deserted garage. Mr. Jones had no chance. Boom! He was dead before his body hit the concrete twenty-two feet away. As soon as the SUV appeared, it disappeared.

Old Hines Plantation

Hines Road

Oakdale

9:20 am

Wednesday

Chris, Jasmine, Mayor Justin Duncan, and Becky met Frank Johnson at the deserted plantation home of General John Hines to explore the possibility of using it as a temporary homeless shelter. A local contractor, Brad Stephens, joined them to offer technical advice on what was needed to get it up to snuff. Becky insisted on going in because she needed a break from mourning her husband's death, overseeing his estate, and all the details that go along with that. Rick had left his estate in good order, but the unending details to manage overwhelmed a now frazzled widow. How to sell his car? What to do with his clothes? His golf clubs? Could she manage the house in Oakdale and keep up the river cottage without him? How will the children do without a dad? The list seemed to go on and on without end. She needed a diversion, so here she was, focused on people experiencing homelessness and how she could help them.

The Hines Plantation is a historic plantation near Oakdale, North Carolina. William Hines originally built it around 1790. The main house is a two-story frame dwelling with exterior gable end brick chimneys featuring Greek Revival period one-story wings and a two-story rear addition. The property also includes a row of frame slave quarters and a stone smokehouse. Bryan Hines, a prominent figure associated with the plantation, was born there in 1828 and later became a Major General in the Confederate Army during the Civil War. The plantation served as his homestead until he died in 1880. The National Register of Historic Places included the property in 1971.

Mr. Johnson bought the property two years earlier from the Hines family with grandiose plans to restore it to its former glory. Although he has not entirely given up on those plans, the sticker shock of the massive restoration project slowed down his enthusiasm. Maybe one day, but for now, he graciously offered it to this rag-tag group to use as a temporary homeless shelter.

The possibilities were enormous. With three and a half bathrooms already in place and six bedrooms, the Hines Plantation offered a solution better than the old National Guard Armory or one of the abandoned tobacco warehouses that they had initially discussed. The biggest issue was the kitchen, which was inadequate to prepare the food necessary to sustain this project. The group received assurance from Brad Stephens, the contractor, that the electrical wiring was usable as he had rewired the home twelve-fifteen years ago. He worried that the HVAC might be a problem, however.

"That will take some money to make it bearable," he said. "And the heating system is an old oil-fired one that is terribly inefficient. I suspect you will need to install a new system for heat and air."

Mayor Duncan, always concerned with the money, piped in, "This is a massive project, one that I want to support. But realistically, I don't think that we can count on much funding from the city. The county and the state may chip in, but not near enough. This will require a major fundraising effort from the community, even though we're getting the house for free."

Looking dejected, Becky and Christina both hung their heads but were not ready to give up.

"Well, let's continue to evaluate the costs before we pass on this," implored Chris.

"Another issue that we need to address, because I'm sure it will come up, is your intentions with the property, Frank. I'm sure that the public funding and private donors will want some assurance that we are not putting a ton of money into this place only to have you pull the rug out from under us in a year or two."

Frank Johnson responded to the thoughtful mayor, "Justin, that's a significant point and one that will certainly need to be ironed out. Before I give you a definitive answer, however, I want to talk to my accountant and my attorney. For now, let's continue in the planning as if we can clear that hurdle."

"I'm not trying to be negative," said the mayor, "but I'm not sure what the neighbors near here will say. I realize that the plantation sits on several acres and is somewhat isolated, but several houses have come along over the years that have this place surrounded by the river."

"That's true too," Becky replied. "So, what does everyone think? Are there too many negatives to go forward? Money? Neighborhood objections? Mr. Johnson's intentions? New kitchen? New HVAC? And we have not even discussed the need for staff, either volunteer or paid. It will take a slew of people to run this place. What does everybody think? Is this worth pursuing, or are we a dog chasing a car with no idea what to do once we catch it?"

The body language of the bunch looked genuinely perplexed, with doubt jumping off their faces. After a long pregnant pause, Jasmine, although not a Biblical scholar, remarkably remembered a scripture that one of her foster parents instilled in her. She spoke up with conviction, reciting Joshua 1:9,

> *'Have I not commanded you? Be strong and courageous. Do not be afraid, do not be discouraged, for the Lord your God will be with you wherever you go.'*

"I'm with Jasmine," said Becky.

Jasmine, quiet until now, felt empowered after Mrs. Baker's three-word affirmation. The company with whom she found herself intimidated her. Just a few weeks ago, she was homeless with no income and one dress to her name. Now, she strutted around an old plantation home with the mayor, an affluent property owner, a former congressman's wife, a pastor's wife, and a general contractor. Although doubtful, it is possible that some of her ancestors were slaves on this very site.

With a newfound confidence, Jasmine continued, "The need is so great. There are veterans, there are good people, and so many who have lost all dignity. And the number is growing. If we can establish a place here where these people feel welcome, where community members can get to know them and realize that they are human beings with hopes and dreams, and where they can get counseling and a hand up, not only will we be helping these down-and-out people, but we will help Oakdale. Mrs. Baker also mentioned the need for staff. I promise you that if you get this place going, it won't be long before the people you are helping get off the street will be the ones staffing the home."

"I feel a strong calling to continue marching until we cannot march anymore," said Chris. "If we allow the Lord to lead us and have the truth on our side, no one or circumstance can stop us."

Slowly, nods began appearing on the rest. Even Mayor Duncan smiled and felt a renewed energy to work on a project that could potentially have a significant positive impact on the town, and reelection was looming.

With an informal consensus achieved, the group dispersed when Chris called everyone back and asked, "Will you pray with me?"

This unlikely group, not all churchgoers, joined hands as Chris prayed,

> *"Almighty God, you are the giver of all gifts, and today we thank you for the gift of a vision to reach out to the least of these and for the resolve that each one here has to help our brothers and sisters. Guide us, oh lord. Direct us. And as Jasmine has quoted from Your Word, keep us strong, courageous, and not discouraged.*
>
> *In Jesus' name, we pray, Amen.*

The inspired individuals left different people than they had been when they arrived. There was a mountain to climb, and each one intended to reach the top, one step at a time.

Oakdale Community Hospital

Friday

10:20 am

Dr. Teesa Williams, a forty-something African American cardiologist, entered Pastor Thornton's room to the delight of both James and Becky. They had high hopes that she would release him and send him home. After a brief greeting and with her head down, focusing on his chart, she looked up, smiled, and said, "Pastor, I'm going to release you today, but only after you promise to adhere to what I have to say to you."

"That sounds great, Doctor; I know I must make some changes."

"Not just some changes, but a whole new lifestyle." In a matter-of-fact tone, all business, and 'serious as a heart attack voice,' she proceeded:" First, you must take all of your medications as prescribed. I have you on blood pressure, cholesterol, blood thinner, and heart function medications. Take them exactly as prescribed. Understood?"

"Yes, ma'am," he responded to the no-frills, all-business doctor.

"Next, I'm referring you to cardiac rehabilitation here at the hospital. They will help you develop an exercise routine, educate you on heart-healthy lifestyle habits, and provide emotional support. You have to fully take part in this program religiously." She grinned when instructing a minister to do something religiously. Maybe there was a personality under her tough façade. "I'm also sending you both to a dietician to learn about a heart-healthy diet. Now, Pastor, I realize this is difficult for a minister, but this is vital. No more banana pudding or fried chicken at The Café, understood?"

"How did you know I ate there?"

"You're a preacher, aren't you?"

"Well, okay. I guess you got me there."

"Now, through this exercise program and an entirely new diet, I expect you to slowly but surely lose weight. I've set a goal for you to lose thirty-five pounds and keep it off. Remember this: if it tastes good, it's not good for you. From here on out, it's fresh vegetables, low sodium, low saturated fat, minimal beef, heavy on fish and chicken, just not fried. You get the idea?"

"Yes, ma'am, you want me to eat cardboard when I'm not exercising."

"Yes, sir, I think you're comprehending. I will give you a written summary of everything I'm saying, but please listen to me on this one. You HAVE to reduce the stress in your life. Many techniques may help you, so when you go to rehab, be sure that you develop a plan with them to reduce stress. It may be a combination of meditation, prayer for sure, deep breathing exercises, and others. They'll work with you on this."

"Okay."

"Pastor, are you a member of any small group through the church? You know, like with fellow pastors."

"I am, but truthfully, I rarely attend those anymore. They've transformed into more gripe sessions than true support groups, as they were originally intended."

"In that case, I want you to join a support group through the hospital with other heart patients. My nurse will help get you the contact information. This is a vital clog in your recovery."

"Okay."

"Finally, Pastor Don, you had a major cardiac event. Nine out of ten people who went through what you did would not be here today. That lady who performed CPR on you saved you. So, from now on, you must know the signs or symptoms of another heart attack. Don't be a typical testosterone-filled male and tough it out. If you have chest pain, shortness of breath, dizziness, or other symptoms, seek medical attention immediately. Mrs. Thornton, be sure he complies with this. I'd much prefer that it's a false alarm than reading your obituary in the Oakdale Times. You both with me on this?"

"Yes, Doc," they both responded in unison.

"The staff will get your paperwork in order, and I suspect you'll be out of here in a couple of hours. Best of luck to you, sir."

"Thank you for everything, Dr. Williams."

Becky added, "If you do not attend a church, we'd love for you to visit ours, Oakdale United Methodist."

Dr. Williams, somewhat stunned because she had never had a white person invite her to church, paused, smiled, and said, "Thank you, Mrs. Thornton. My wife and I do not attend church regularly, so I'll tell her about your kind invitation. In the meantime, let's get Mr. Thornton home and on with his recovery."

The shock of Reverend Thornton hearing that this brilliant doctor, who made all the right moves to save him, is not only black but also gay. He thought about his 'conversation' with Jesus while unconscious, smiled back, and said, "We'd love to have you both.

FBI Headquarters

J. Edgar Hoover Building

935 Pennsylvania Avenue

Washington, DC

Monday 11:05 am

A giddy Daryl Bonner, a data scientist for Data Analytics Group (DAG), knocked on Tom Murray's office in the FBI headquarters building. Tom, an up-and-coming special agent, had been on the job about as long as Daryl, both about two years. Daryl earned a Bachelor of Science (BS) degree in Computer Science from the University of

Virginia and a Master of Engineering (ME) in Systems Engineering, also from UVA. Several companies heavily recruited him in the DC area, the Research Triangle Park in North Carolina, and Silicon Valley. He chose DAG because of the projects they were working on with the U.S. government, which seemed to Daryl to be exciting, current, and of utmost importance to our national security. As with many new employees, his first two years were less than thrilling. He seemed to get projects that no one else wanted. He kept telling himself that this would pass and once he learned the company's culture, the lingo, and their specific software and its capabilities, he would move up to the exciting projects that lured him to DAG. His last assignment, tracking correlations between people vaccinated for COVID and their outcomes, although not exciting, was critical, and Daryl jumped into that headfirst. His assignment to track down what appeared to be a prostitute extorting money from a naïve congressman seemed like a dead-end waste of time. Thus, his supervisor gave it to him. But maybe, just maybe, this case was more than what appeared. Tom sensed the excitement in Daryl's face, as much as a data scientist dared show.

"What'd you got?" asked Tom

You remember the project that you outsourced to DAG about the mysterious lady that Congressman wrote about and sent pictures of before he committed suicide?"

"Sure, what'd find?"

"I spent all weekend here working with the Bureau's system, trying to uncover any clues about her. There was nothing. So, I ran some face detection programs using the pictures the congressman sent you. With that as the control shot, I compared it to every function the congressman had been to the previous month, including his funeral. You will not believe this, but I had matches at the function for the Taiwanese chip facility possibly coming to the USA and his funeral. She actually went to his funeral!"

"Who is she?"

"That's the intriguing part. She does not exist."

"What?"

"I found no record of her attending the chip function. None. I have no idea how she got in."

"Interesting. Let me look at my notes. Yes, here. Congressman Davis said that her name was Aleksandre Wojic."

Yes, so I searched every database known to the FBI that my security clearance allowed. Nothing. I'm telling you, she doesn't exist."

Special Agent Bonner mused the new information, thinking out loud, "Okay, we have a gorgeous lady who somehow crashed the chip reception, seduced a country doctor congressman, blackmailed him for money or maybe for something else, maybe votes, and was crazy enough to go to his funeral. I've dealt with foreign agents in cooperation with the CIA, and a Russian agent would not make that mistake. Is it possible that they had a long-time affair?"

"According to my data, she never showed up before or since this incident, so it appears doubtful."

Again, thinking out loud, "So who is she, who employed her, and where is she now?"

"That is what I don't know. I know that her face did not appear in any of the thousands of photographs taken at congressional or White House functions. I even searched photographs from the congressman's files that we have stored on the system, but nothing was found from his district gatherings. I'm telling you, Tom, she does not exist. Just between us, does this sound like a Russian agent?"

"It's possible, Daryl. I think I'll refer this data to my friend at the CIA and see if those guys want to pursue it. This is intriguing, but it remains to be seen if this data will work its way up to a point where someone truly investigates it or if it will be buried along with thousands of other lower-level investigations. Daryl, this is great work. Thank you."

"I hope that it helps."

"By the way, since you have Top Secret security clearance, I'll just mention that we have pulled the bodyguards from Congressman Davis's family. With him dead and no longer under the influence of any blackmailer, extortionist, or anybody, the risk to them seems remote. Also, keep this under your hat, but we've received a referral from the DC police that a custodian killed in a hit-and-run in the Cannon Building parking lot may be more than an accident. We don't know if it's connected to the situation with the congressman, but at least someone has verbalized the idea.

"Thanks, Tom. Let me know if DAG can help with this investigation anymore."

"Will do. See you, buddy."

"Alright, take care."

Oakdale United Methodist Church

Oakdale, NC

Sunday

9:30 am

Another beautiful day in Oakdale started much the same as any Sunday for the small congregation attending Oakdale UMC. People trickled in starting at 9:00 am, but most hustled to the Fellowship Hall at 9:25 am or later. Adult Sunday School begins at 9:30 am, or at least that was the advertised time. In reality, with people coming in at precisely 9:30 am and some later, the conversations continued until finally, at 9:38 am, the leader, Delores Pritchard, opened the class with a short prayer. Delores read the Bible more than anyone in the church. Instead of reading novels, biographies, or even news articles, she read the Bible. She preyed on her obvious superiority of Biblical teachings to the point that she skewed them to meet her agenda. Her know-it-all personality, particularly about the

Bible, stifled discussion and virtually stopped debate or other opinions. Yet, people came every Sunday to her class. This Sunday, as with most classes, she started by informing the class that she did not know what the lesson would be as she drove to the church and would let God lead her once she arrived. This was fine, but the lesson typically lacked structure, resulting in her rambling about a particular subject. Behind her back, some attendees discussed her teaching style and suggested that she allow God to give her the lesson on Tuesday or Wednesday, thus providing time for her to prepare a well-planned lesson. She'd taught the class for years, and no one else ever volunteered to teach it, so the congregation put up with her unorganized approach and were grateful that she would do it. If she didn't, there would be no Sunday School class.

The worship service also started as it had for years, with the same order of worship, the same songs, the same everything. Then it changed. Pastor Don Thornton stood behind the pulpit for the first time since his heart attack. A buzz filled the sanctuary as the congregants anxiously awaited to hear from their beloved orator. His voice was weak, he was pale, and he had lost some weight. What changed, however, was his message.

"Good morning, dear brothers and sisters in Christ. First, thank you! Thank you sincerely for your prayers, concerns, and food, and to all who have stepped up to keep the church going and to those who filled in this pulpit to preach during my absence. Both Christina and I sincerely appreciate your love and caring. Although I have

personally thanked them, let me publicly express my gratitude to Jasmine and Mia for their quick action on that day when I had a heart attack out here. I've had several doctors tell me that I would not be here had it not been for Jasmine's quick action.

As a result of this incident and because we are getting older, Chris and I have been talking a lot lately about the hereafter. Just last night, I walked into the kitchen and asked Chris, 'What am I in hereafter?'" After some polite chuckling, the pastor continued.

"As many of you know, during my unconscious state, I had a powerful encounter with our Lord and Savior, Jesus Christ. I must confess, He expressed displeasure with what I was doing at this church, and He was not happy with what we as a congregation were doing. He told me that I, and you, were going through the motions. Yes, we attend faithfully, yes, we give tithes and offerings faithfully, and yes, He was pleased with the ministries that we have been carrying out for years. My friends, He made it very clear, however, that we were not doing enough. He clearly communicated that our efforts were insufficient to make disciples for Him and for us to reach out to the poor, the lost, the lonely, the elderly, and the homeless. We have not shouted from the rooftops what the love of Jesus Christ is all about.

Brothers and sisters, as clear as I see you here today, I saw Jesus. It was real. I know that I'm stepping on toes here today, but believe me, Jesus stomped on my toes. He told me that we were focused on the wrong issues.

Think about how much time and effort we had spent talking to each other, making calls, and soliciting support to leave the United Methodist Church because of the issue of human sexuality. I'm not here to debate with you the theology behind this dividing issue, but what I am here to tell you is that Jesus said to me that all people are His people. We are not to judge; He will do that. Our responsibility is to love our neighbors as ourselves. Spread the love of Jesus to everyone, not just those that look like us. He wants us to be inclusive, not exclusive. We are not a social club whereby we vote to allow people in. Instead of being a country club, we are something else. We are a hospital for sinners, and He wants us not only to welcome all but to reach out to all and bring them into the church. He wants us to serve others, not the other way around.

I realize that faith is the cornerstone of our lives. Without faith, we have nothing. But Jesus clarified that faith alone is not enough; action must accompany it. You heard the words from Matthew 25:40 read today. We are called to focus on 'the least of these brothers and sisters of mine.' Jesus made it clear in James 2:14-17 that faith alone is not enough; action must accompany it. Hear these words from Jesus, "What good is it, my brothers, if someone says that he has faith but does not have works? Can that faith save him? If a brother or sister is poorly clothed and lacking in daily food, and one of you says to them, 'Go in peace, be warmed and filled, without giving them the things needed for the body, what good is that? So also, faith by itself, if it does not have works, is dead."

I confess to you today that I have had scripture in my mouth and hate in my heart. I have not reached out to the black community, the homeless people, or to the LGBTQIA+ community. I did not welcome Jasmine and Mia as I should have. I have not been to the overpass to minister to the homeless congregated there. I have not ministered to the prisoners. I have not supported the local soup kitchen to the degree I can. I have not volunteered at the hospital unless one of you was there. I have not become involved in community programs to help immigrants and refugees. My question to you is, 'Have you? Have you?

I realize I have crossed the line from preaching to meddling for some of you. But my friends, Jesus is real. He told me what to do. Quite frankly, he got my attention. Yes, what I'm suggesting is overwhelming. Yes, it is outside of many of our comfort zones. I suspect that we may lose a few of you to other churches. But I have no choice; this is what Jesus Himself instructed me to do and what I plan to do with all the vigor and focus every day that He allows me to stay on this earth. I pray that you will join me. Remember the promise in Galicians 6:9, 'And let us not grow weary of doing good, for in due season we will reap if we do not give up.' God equips us with the strength and resources we need to serve others.

So, as I stand here today, renewed in spirit and purpose, I invite you all to join me in this divine mission. Let us be a church that not only professes faith in Jesus but also lives out His teachings through our actions.

Remember, in serving others, we are serving Christ Himself.

Let us pray: Dear Heavenly Father, You are the giver of all gifts, and we thank You for the gift of faith and the call to action. Strengthen us to serve 'the least of these' with love and compassion. May our actions reflect Your love and bring glory to Your name. In Jesus' name, we pray. Amen"

The congregation filed out as always, shaking hands with the pastor. They had heard sermons about "The Least of These Brothers" before, but this one seemed different. Even though Pastor Don was weak and not as adamant as usual, his sense of conviction seemed off the charts today. Some found themselves energized, but others began to think that this was not what they had signed up for upon joining the church. They were not yet ready to welcome blacks, Hispanics, LGBTQIA+, homeless, or really anyone who didn't look like them. Pastor Don's resolve surely was about to be tested, and he knew it. But he also knew what Jesus told him in no uncertain terms. He had no choice. The church would change, or they would move him to another appointment in another town come July 1st, just like they had done so many before him.

Jasmine and Mia left, grinning from ear to ear. They believed the pastor was sincere, and they were both ready to help with his new vision cast by Jesus. They thanked Reverend Thornton on their way out and waited for his wife, Christina, to drive them back to the parsonage, where they continued to stay.

The shock of the day for Pastor Don was not so much who left excited, intimidated, or disgusted, but the fact two African American women, Dr. Teesa Williams, his brilliant cardiologist, and her wife, Bess McDavid, attended the service. As they passed through the line shaking hands with the pastor, Dr. Williams gave Don a firm handshake, introduced him to her wife Bess, and said, "Pastor Thornton, I'm delighted that you can physically be back in the pulpit today, and I'm ecstatic with your sermon. I hope that you will have the resolve to stand up for your newfound convictions. But please, don't overdo it just yet. Build back your strength."

"Spoken like a true doctor," he replied. "And thank you for coming. Your presence here today will help with the positive changes that I envision. Nice to meet you, Bess. Please come back."

Croatan County Courthouse

City Council Room

Tuesday

7:20 pm

Frank Johnson attended the City Council meeting along with a contingency of advocates for a new homeless shelter in Oakdale. Christina, Becky, Jasmine, Pastor Don, and others sat patiently waiting for the Council to take up their request to rezone the old Hines Plantation home to allow for a homeless shelter.

The topic ahead of them consisted of a farmer who had planned to expand his hog farm to a new location, one on the outskirts of town in the general vicinity of a new subdivision that had popped up over the last few years. Several residents of the subdivision came to protest the rezoning request and block the creation of the hog farm. An affluent and well-respected attorney from Oakdale represented the opposition. Dressed in a beautifully tailored suit, he started his well-thought-out, well-researched bullet points against the farm. He presented a long list of reasons why the permit for the hog farm should be denied. In the time allowed, the lawyer discussed environmental concerns, including contamination of local rivers and streams because of the runoff of waste and chemicals. Next, he addressed Air Quality degradation from foul odors, ammonia, and methane, which could pose health risks. Public health risks such as respiratory problems, infections, the potential spread of diseases from hogs to humans like Swine Flu, pest infestation, particularly flies and rodents that could spread disease. The lawyer continued without so much as a quick breath, talking about noise pollution from the animals, machinery, and transport vehicles, thus disrupting the peace the residents had grown accustomed to and loved. He spoke of decreasing property values, the negative visual impact on the landscape, increased wear and tear on the local roads caused by heavy trucks, and potential harm to local wildlife habitats and ecosystems from pollution and habitat destruction. The attorney nailed it. His case for blocking the hog farm was impenetrable.

Next up was the farmer, an uneducated, sixty-two-year-old man dressed in overalls, who had long, disheveled hair pouring out the sides and back of a ball cap advertising a local fertilizer company. He scanned the nine council members and Mayor Duncan, with only one point to argue for his case. "We're talkin' 'bout hogs. They're just hogs. It's not like I'm trying to bring in busloads of Yankees to live here. It's just hogs." Mayor Duncan tried to quiet the laughter from all corners of the room, but this was too good to stifle. After the room quieted, they voted eight to one to allow the hog farm. The only dissenting vote came from the councilman from the district where the proposed farm would be.

Mayor Duncan introduced the next item on the agenda: the request to rezone the old Hines Planation house so that a homeless shelter can operate there.

After consulting with his accountant and attorney, Mr. Johnson, the owner of the Hines Plantation, devised a plan in which they could use the house as a homeless shelter without him permanently relinquishing total control. He offered the plantation to the group organizing the shelter, at no charge, as a Determinable Fee Simple. This way, the recipient is granted the property for as long as they use it for a specified purpose. Ownership automatically reverts to the original owner (Mr. Johnson or his heirs) if the property ceases to be used for the specified purpose. This was perfect for both groups. The shelter committee formed a legal entity known as a Limited Liability Corporation (LLC) so that the LLC, not the individuals, owned the shelter. Thus, any lawsuits because of anything that happened on the property would have to be brought against the LLC, not the organizers personally. They are free to upgrade the property, and it will remain in their possession as long as they use it for a homeless shelter. Mr. Johnson specified in the legal documents that the organizers are responsible for making any improvements or changes to the property and outlying building in a manner that upholds the historical integrity of the plantation. The committee agreed with that wholeheartedly. With that hurdle jumped, now they had to obtain approval from the City Council to allow such an operation.

Mayor Duncan called for a representative of the group to make their case for the shelter. Since the mayor was on board with the idea from its inception, he had called each of the other council members in advance, explaining how this would remove the eyesore of the encampment from under the overpass, the unofficial entrance to the town. They all liked the idea since they were getting flak from their constituents over the unsightly mess. The house, although near town, was on enough acreage that there weren't any houses close to the plantation home, but a few had inched their way into the general vicinity over the years. Christina made the initial presentation by discussing how the home would provide a second chance for people needing a hand-up. She mentioned the sadness that many veterans were now living in the encampment and that the community could do better than allowing those who served us in foreign lands to live in a tent beside the road. She talked about the plans to solicit doctors, mental health professionals, churches, job placement personnel, attorneys, and others as needed to donate time and resources to get these folks back on their feet and become assets to the community instead of a drain. The council members all nodded in agreement as she talked. Only two raised their hands upon Mayor Duncan's call for anyone to speak against the project. Both were neighbors in the sense that their homes were in the vicinity. Both feared that crime would increase and that they would no longer feel safe in their homes. Mayor Duncan called for the vote—nine to zero in favor of the shelter. The delighted committee members left the meeting with smiles and a feeling of accomplishment. They also felt a two-ton weight on their shoulders. What would they do now that the project was indeed up and going?

Home of Becky Davis

Greendale Acres

Oakdale

Sunday Night

Becky had put on a strong face in public since the suicide of her husband and only actual boyfriend since high school, Dr. Rick Davis. There were so many unanswered questions, and she realized that the questions would remain unanswered forever. Why did he do it? Was I to blame? Did I nag him too much to come home more, be with the three young sons more, be a husband occasionally instead of a U.S. congressman 24/7? What precipitated his demise? Is it possible that it wasn't suicide but a murder, maybe by some evil force trying to take over the country from within? What was the money in foreign accounts all about? Where did he get it? Why an offshore account? Why had he not mentioned it to me? Who was the stranger, a beautiful lady who attended his funeral? She was not a local nor a staff member. Her mind raced. No matter how hard she tried, she could not expel these questions from consuming her brain. She tried a glass or two of wine. No help. A tranquilizer during the roughest times helped, but it was only a band-aid and did not address the underlying questions. The questions. They would not go away. There are too many questions, not just too few, but no answers. She felt as if her brain was exploding, and she had no way to defuse it. So, she cried. She cried a lot. After getting the boys to bed, which was a real challenge because they, too, were dealing with the death of their dad, she cried. Her only diversion that seemed to help and that made the questions vanish, if only for short periods, was her work at the homeless shelter. She told no one, but that effort, intended to help the lost souls living under an overpass, actually helped her more than anything that she did for them. She needed a therapist. That was clear. No one would blame her. Her closest friends encouraged it, but the stigma of seeing a shrink caused her not to pull the trigger. But she knew—she knew—that she needed help, and something had to give soon. So, she cried.

Added to her anxiety were the boys and their mental health. The youngest two seemed to cope as well as expected after their hero, their invincible dad had died, and they would never see him again. Their three-year-old, Mason, sat at the window every afternoon waiting for his dad to drive up. The fact that Rick had spent so much time in Washington, DC, weirdly, helped because the boys had learned a routine and a life that did not include their dad as much as other kids' dads. The seven-year-old, Noah, understood better that their dad would never drive into the driveway again. The entire family's exhilaration when they heard the garage door open and Rick parked his SUV was history, never to be felt again. And he cried. He and Mason both acted out their grief with unacceptable behavior; pitching fits, obstinate actions never seen by Becky, refusal to take baths without a fight, refusal to eat, throwing their food off of the table, screaming at their mom, and rarely laughing or even smiling. Noah's second-grade teacher called Becky, informing her of his downward spiral in school. He was not the same happy, eager-to-experience-new adventures kid as he was before his dad's death. As bad as it was for Mason and Noah, Ethan's issue was ten times worse. As a result of the kidnapping, he remained petrified. He never rode his bike to school or anywhere unless he had his mom with him. He refused to go outside by himself. He feared everyone. His teacher also had several conversations with Becky, expressing her deep concerns about him. Now, on top of that trauma, add the fact that his dad was dead. Ethan was old enough to read the papers. He understood that his dad shot himself. Ethan blamed himself. Perhaps the reason his dad killed himself was because of his kidnapping. Maybe he had not been a good enough son. Maybe he disappointed his dad by not being an outstanding athlete like his dad was, or as smart in school as his dad. Ethan knew more than his two younger brothers, that his dad would never show up at any of his Little League games or school programs, pull him tubing at the river cottage, or take him fishing or crabbing. His dad never would tell corny ghost stories around a campfire eating smores at the river. His dad was gone. So, most nights, Ethan, just like his mom, cried himself to sleep.

Hines Plantation

Oakdale

Tuesday

The committee members had already made much progress with the meager funds they could solicit. The kitchen was gutted, electrical systems were checked and approved, and the basic plumbing was in working order. Thankfully, the plantation's connection to the Oakdale city sewage system years ago meant that there were no issues with a septic system handling the anticipated dramatic increase in water usage. So far, local contractors have donated the work, but the kitchen would require a significant investment that no contractor was willing or able to swallow. The project required more funding. Through donations from area churches, cots, bed linens, and towels were procured. Local landscapers and volunteers had made tremendous progress in reviving the landscaping to its original glory.

This dog was close to catching the car, so it was time to get real with how this shelter was to be run. Many rules, structure, and expectations of the staff, volunteers, and particularly the guests, needed to be planned. We are implementing the effective strategies developed by Ed Murphy at All God's Children in Philadelphia, and we are also motivated by Pastor Don's first sermon after his heart attack. The committee planned to focus their efforts on the words of Jesus as written in Matthew 25, which said that by welcoming the "least of these," the hungry, the thirsty, and the naked, they would indeed welcome Jesus Himself. This place will offer the oppressed in the community a place to sleep and eat, a bathroom, a shower, a phone, a place to wash clothes, and a place to receive mail. The home will be Christ-centered, with Bible studies, a Sunday service, and prayers before each meal. To stay at the plantation, the guests, even non-believers, must attend the services. The organizers knew well that they would not convert people to Christ but left that chore to God. They simply planned to put the lost into a situation whereby God could do His work.

Everyone on the plantation was to wear name tags, including the guests, the staff, and all the volunteers. Everyone was to be treated with love and respect. Pastor Don insisted on this and set the tone every chance that he had, emphasizing that, "These are people. Pastor Don insisted on treating everyone with love and respect, emphasizing that they are people, regardless of their race, education, or any drug or alcohol issues they may have. It's our job to treat them as such. Unlike the Soup Kitchen, which lines up the people to receive their food and sends them on their way, we here at the plantation will call our guests by name. We will treat them as guests, sincerely ask about their day, and sit and eat with them, talk to them, and listen. The personal touch will set us apart and help turn around lives. With God's help, we will personally know everyone coming through these doors, fostering a deep sense of empathy and connection.

Ed instilled in the Oakdale committee that their experience in Philadelphia was that in meeting Christ in the homeless people, we, the givers, experience renewed life and joy, along with a heartache that reflects the cross. According to Ed, "The life and joy come from the patience, goodness, and humor exhibited by the homeless that now live at All God's Children. Before long, you will find that the homeless people will share their stories, hopes, and dreams with the staff and volunteers. The gifts we discover in these people are phenomenal, bringing a sense of fulfillment and joy in serving others.

So, with high expectations and much trepidation, Jasmine and Christina took the church van to bring people to the plantation. It wasn't ready to provide home-cooked meals, but at least it could start by providing shelter, showers, and bathrooms. Although Jasmine did not feel comfortable playing God by arbitrarily choosing who could go and who could not, she did her best in a caring and loving way. Women and children took priority. They brought six people on the first run and returned to get six more. Volunteers awaited these first residents of the plantation, offering food donated from a couple of local restaurants, name tags, towels, soap, and other toiletries. For some it was like Christmas morning, only better. The volunteers assigned rooms based on need. The volunteers assigned some individuals to cots placed in the former living room while they gave bedrooms to others. They also had clean beds ready for a few individuals in the old slave quarters of the plantation. The people in the slave quarters did not have bathrooms other than a four-seater outhouse that remained from the days of slavery, but they had access to the bathrooms in the main house at any time. An outdoor shower was available for a quick rinse down, but the showers inside were also available to all on a schedule posted by each shower. A new life had begun, one with caring, God-loving people there to guide, aid, teach, and love them. Mayor Justin Duncan welcomed each person to the facility and thanked all the volunteers who worked diligently to prepare the house. Much was yet to do, but the house was open and beginning its work. Halleluiah!

Oakdale UMC Parsonage

Thursday

6:15 pm

Christina and Don just finished their supper; a small piece of baked chicken, steamed broccoli, boiled carrots, and unsweet decaffeinated iced tea. Chris gave him a no-sugar cherry-flavored gelatin dessert as if that may satisfy his sweet tooth. Not even close. He spooned the last bite into his mouth, looked at Chris, and said with a smile, "That was not a bad appetizer. What are we having for supper?" She couldn't help but laugh, considering what he was used to devouring before his heart attack. No apple pie a la mode for the starving pastor tonight. But he knew what he had to do and thanked Chris for helping him stay on track.

Chris gathered a few files and her keys and scurried out to attend choir practice at the church. Don sat in his recliner alone and thought about his lifelong buddy, Rick. Don had not come to grips yet that Rick was gone. His best friend since Little League Baseball is gone, never to be seen again. Questions consumed him just like they had Becky and their sons. "Why did he do this? Why didn't he come to me? I'm a counselor and his best friend. No more golf with him, no more Saturday night dinners, no more helping each other with minor projects around the houses, no more working together on the issues we both embraced. Oh, how I wish I could tell him about my encounter with Christ. I so wish that he could see the new me, the one now working for the homeless people and not just running them off of the streets. I want to tell him how I've changed regarding the human sexuality issue with the United Methodist Church. I want to introduce him to Dr. Williams and her wife. I ache for my friend." Tears flowed as he thought of Becky and the three sons. "What would they do? How would they fare without their dad and husband?" He never had a chance to say goodbye because he was in the hospital while his friend's funeral took place. More tears poured down his face, and he uncontrollably started crying out loud. His sobbing was no less loud than a hungry baby screaming for food. In the middle of his release of pent-up emotions, his mode changed. He went from mourning to anger. "How could he do this to his family? How could he do this to his community and constituents? How could he do this to me?"

Before his heart attack, Pastor Don would have darted to the cupboard and poured a stiff drink of bourbon, but now he resisted the temptation and cried until there were no more tears. He needed this time to let go. He still had a way to go before he could be even close to overcoming the loss of his friend, but finally, this was a good first step.

Hines Plantation

Oakdale

Saturday

9:20 am

The first few nights with residents at the Hines Plantation went well, but not without a few hitches. In this place, where much is given, the residents soon realized that there are also high expectations. Food was still being brought in, donated by local restaurants, but everyone knew that it was not the long-term answer. Two of the restaurants had already given notice that they could not continue with their generosity for more than a couple of weeks. The work on the kitchen continued, but then again, the volunteer workers were getting tired and ready to return to their everyday lives. The professionals who donated their time, expertise, and sometimes their materials also grew weary of the project's magnitude, and their paying customers were becoming less and less patient.

Some residents eagerly identified daily tasks that needed completion, but some still wanted to lie back and let others do the work while they received the benefits. One resident, a young female with obvious addiction problems, had a six-pack of beer in her room. Although she did not cause a disturbance, was discreet, and drank it privately, the still-learning management team felt that they could not budge on the rule prohibiting alcohol or illegal drugs on the premises and evicted her. This tore at the heartstrings of

Life Goes On

everyone, but they knew that this was necessary. They gave her room to two residents living in the slave quarters, and another homeless person from the overpass took the slave quarter spot. Tough love had to be adhered to. The staff treated the abuser of the alcohol rule with respect and instructed her to reapply for residency in thirty days.

The plan to bring much-needed medical help started immediately. A local doctor spent an entire day with his nurse evaluating the residents. Most were malnourished or suffered from minor infections and cuts and scrapes from altercations with other homeless people. Some, however, faced much more challenging health problems. Joe, a black veteran who served in the Marines during the Vietnam War, had multiple issues identified by the doctor. In addition to malnutrition, Joe had lice and probably trench foot. The doctor's primary concern was mental illness, more so than his obvious physical abnormalities. He suffered from anxiety, depression, and possibly PTSD (Post-Traumatic Stress Disorder). The good Doc placed Joe on the referral list to receive mental health services. In one day of volunteering, the doctor identified people with untreated diabetes, respiratory infections, and many suffering from mental health issues that needed immediate attention. Of course, the connection between physical problems and mental health was obvious to the doctor. The doctor needed to provide a lot of care and left feeling overwhelmed, saddened, and without many answers. Most of the residents had no medical insurance, no money, and were forced to live with their untreated illnesses.

Money, as with most initiatives, would help, but without it, the entire dream of Christina Thornton, Becky Davis, and the others would soon become a nightmare. Mayor Duncan obtained $10,000 for the cause through the City of Oakdale, and the County also found $10,000 in their budget to donate. There were generous donations from individuals and local businesspeople, all of which were appreciated. It became rapidly apparent, however, that this undertaking would require much more. The funds secured thus far would not provide enough to complete the needed home renovations, much less to pay for the food and ongoing medical care. A dejected group left the Plantation late Saturday afternoon. They were pleased to hear the gratitude of the residents, to see them clean and fed for the first time in years for some, but they were more than concerned that they had bitten off more than they could chew.

As the volunteers departed for their homes, apart from those who agreed to stay the night, Mia, of all people, once again, achieved a remarkable impact, exceeding what is typically expected from an eight-year-old. She had organized three of the kids on the site along with four adults, and out of nowhere, began singing with beautiful a cappella voices, in harmony laden with soul and in the gospel tradition of Black churches:

"Great is Thy faithfulness! Great is Thy faithfulness!

Morning by morning, new mercies I see;

All I have needed, Thy hand hath provided---

Great is Thy faithfulness, Lord, unto me!

Everything changed, and hope rose to the top. The mountain was still high, but the resolve of one step at a time, trusting the Lord to provide, overtook the dejected organizers, and hope smothered the growing doubts.

Oakdale UMC

Fellowship Hall

Sunday

2:00 pm

Administrative Council Chairman, John Brewbaker, called a special council meeting. He allowed the council members time to go to The Café for lunch, as was the tradition, before convening the meeting. Much parking lot talk necessitated the meeting, and Mr. Brewbaker believed that the best approach was to meet the scuttlebutt head-on. Besides the treasurer, the Lay Leader, and the Chairman of the Staff Parish Relations Committee, a few members of the congregation were present. Mr. Brewbaker opened with a prayer, but it wasn't long before these devout Christians' reverent and communal mood changed. Although there was no cussing, there might as well have been. Many in the congregation seemed to have steam bellowing from both ears when they saw Pastor Don unloading homeless people from the church van before the morning worship and parading them into the sanctuary. Drug addicts, alcoholics, and nasty-looking creatures in ragged clothes, unshaven, and no showers in recent memory filed into the once revered sanctuary. Murmurs prevailed throughout the beautifully adorned sanctuary with antique stained-glass windows, allowing the morning light to filter in. "What kind of stunt is this? What is happening to our church? The pastor must have lost his mind when in the hospital. He never would have allowed this before. Now, he's the one going to pick up these derelicts. We must put a stop to this, and I mean now." On and on went the whispers throughout the entire service. Very few heard a word of Reverend Thorton's sermon on love as their anger increased.

"First, he nixed the idea of disaffiliation from the United Methodist Church," one long-time member almost shouted and was upset to the point of disgust. "Next, he invited those black lesbians to attend, and they were back today. Now he's hauling every thief, rapist, and murderer he can find into our beloved place of worship."

More chimed in, just as disgusted. The holy, peaceful, loving people of God had more than a few choice words for their once-beloved pastor and friend.

Pastor Thornton, when this bashing was taking place, was back at the overpass where he gathered as many of the homeless and lost souls as he could, those not yet fortunate to move out to the Plantation and had a church service right there as the cars whizzed by above. His voice was not yet back to pre-heart attack levels, but the ten or twelve that gathered moved in closer as he spoke. Mia's makeshift choir led the group in singing. Pastor Don offered the listeners hope through the love of Jesus Christ. He knew that it would take more than one sermon to convert any of these people, as they had not felt the love of Jesus for years, if ever. Their lives all went south for different reasons, and they did not think that an invisible myth from two thousand years ago would help them. But for Pastor Don, it was another step to work on the mission that Jesus ordered him to pursue. He refused to be discouraged. He promised that he would be back next week and every week.

Clyde Woodruff and his wife Vivian, long-time members of the Oakdale UMC, as were his parents and grandparents, were the first to explode after hearing several at the special meeting express their disgust. "I can't take this place anymore," he proclaimed. "Vivian and I are leaving and will find another church that believes in the Bible and does not cozy up to these perverts. And we're taking our money with us!" He and Vivian left and slammed the door on the way out. He was by far the largest donor to the church, so when he and his money left, a sizeable chunk of the annual budget left with him. Others followed. Some, however, the less vocal ones, stayed. The Lay Leader, Charles Humphries, tried to make a counterpoint to those remaining talking about Matthew 25 and the preacher's sermon when he returned from his hospital stay. Others just sat there in a reflective posture. What would become of this church without the Woodruff money, and is the addition of these "least of these" truly what Jesus wants for this church?

After the meeting, phones rang throughout the congregation. One would have thought that the church was on fire at how word spread of the meeting and Mr. Woodruff's threat that seemed more than a threat. Word soon came to Pastor Don as well. Although disappointed with some congregants' reaction, Mr. Woodruff's threat did not deter him. Was he going to listen to Clyde, or would he listen to Jesus? He pulled up his britches, pulled back his shoulders, stuck out his chest, and vowed not to stop charging. In his car, pulled over to the side of the road, he prayed. He prayed for perseverance through this storm.

Offices of McGann, Newman, and Sampson

Attorneys at Law

Oakdale Business District

Monday

10:20 am

"Hello, Newman," said a playful Becky as she entered the law office of Mr. Brian Newman, a long-time family friend and the Davis family attorney. Brian smiled back and gave her a slight nod, knowing she loved referencing the Newman in Seinfeld. It annoyed Brian because virtually everyone, at least the Seinfeld fans, did the same greeting. This was Becky, so it didn't bother him.

He jumped right into the reason for the visit, however, because he had other clients and much work to do.

"Becky, I looked into Rick's accounts in the Cayman Islands. Did you know about them?"

"No."

"Well, I cannot discern where the money came from, but he made sporadic deposits over a period that started shortly after his election to the Congress. $10,000 here, $50,000 there over the last few years. He never made a withdrawal."

"How much is in the accounts?"

"Just shy of $750,000."

"750,000 dollars? she exclaimed.

"Yes."

"Holy mackerel. Brian! Where in the world did he come up with that kind of money?"

"I don't know Becky. I've been his attorney for years, handled every real estate transaction, did all of his legal work, and never did he mention anything like this."

"I'm his fricking wife, and he never said a word to me either. Well, can you transfer the money to my account with United Bank?"

"It's not that easy, Becky. First, the offshore bank will require identification documents, proof of address, and account ownership documents. I believe he gave you the location of the account ownership documents in his letter, correct?"

"Yes, he did."

Okay, next, you need to know that if these funds were obtained illegally and not reported, transferring them could cause severe problems for you. The U.S. has strict regulations regarding money laundering and tax evasion. And helping you could put me at risk as well. He should have filed reports to the IRS, such as FBAR (Report of Foreign Bank and Financial Accounts) and FATCA (Foreign Account Tax Compliance Act). With your approval, I'll confidently call your accountant to confirm, but I'll bet that nobody has filed any of these forms."

"Yes, please call him. I trust him just as I do you."

"If all is on the up and up, we can initiate a transfer or a series of transfers. We'll need some information from you and there may be some fees, but we can handle all that, no problem. There are several ways to transfer the money, but let's not get ahead of our skis just yet." Brian took off his glasses, looked Becky in the eyes, and said with a solemn face, "Becky, you are in a tough spot. If you declare this money to the IRS as required, it will probably trigger an investigation by the FBI. How did a U.S. congressman accumulate that kind of money? Why did he hide it in a foreign account? Why did he not tell his accountant, attorney, or wife about it? Does this have anything to do with his suicide? Do you see where I'm going? I'm not sure what liability you have. I'll have to study that some more.

But at the very least, his name and reputation will probably be disgraced. On the other hand, if we can figure out a way to get you the money in small increments, it may fly under the radar, but this is risky."

"I could shoot that sorry bum if he hadn't already done it," she laments. "He's put me in a terrible spot. Brian, what if the money does not come to me but to a charity here in the States?"

"That's an interesting thought. The donation would offset the income, so there may not be any tax consequences. I have an idea, but I need to research it more. I have a junior associate in the office who is a whiz with cryptocurrency. Maybe we can convert the money to Bitcoin or some other cryptocurrency and transfer it to a personal wallet, where you can withdraw it at your discretion.

"All of this is way over my head, but I have decided that if we can get the funds transferred, I want it to go to a charity, one that I have in mind. I don't want a single penny of his ill-gotten fortune."

"Becky, I know you're a religious person. Go home and pray about this. In the meantime, I'll do some homework to see how we can get the money to where you want it to go."

"Okay, thank you, Brian."

"I'll get back to you soon."

Hines Plantation

Oakdale

Saturday

7:00 am

Oakdale police quietly surrounded the perimeter of the Hines Plantation as two detectives pounded on the front door. A petrified volunteer who had spent the night with the residents opened the front door with her heart pounding out of her chest. In ill-fitting sports coats and ties not quite up to their necks, the two overweight detectives quickly flashed their badges as they barged into the foyer.

"Wait, what are you doing? What's going on?" pleaded the volunteer.

"We have a search warrant and are here to search the premises for stolen goods. There has been a rash of robberies nearby, and we have reason to believe that one or more of these degenerates living here is to blame. So, you step aside and let us do our work."

Behind the detectives, four uniformed policemen rolled in and spread out throughout the house, going from room to room, looking for the contraband. They startled several still-sleeping residents, who immediately took up self-defense positions. Most of these homeless people were no strangers to the police, sometimes warranted and sometimes not. But they all knew that their best bet was to step aside, be quiet, and let the zealous police officers do whatever they were doing. The searchers scrambled whatever personal items were in the rooms, with no attempt to keep any order. After leaving a mess, they looked under the beds and retreated to another room to destroy it.

The horrified volunteer immediately called Christine who in turn woke up Mayor Duncan. The mayor knew nothing of the raid and was livid upon hearing the news. First, he missed the last and most satisfying part of his beauty sleep, but why was his police out there harassing the residents, particularly without his knowledge? After a quick trip to the bathroom, he threw on a pair of khakis and whatever shirt he could find and took off to the house. On his way, he called the police chief, wanting some answers and wanting them now. The not-so-stupid police chief had better sense than to answer the phone from the mayor at that hour of the morning, so he escaped a major tongue-lashing first thing that Saturday morning. By the time Mayor Duncan arrived at the house, the police were winding up their search, having found nothing but leaving the house in total disarray. The mayor went directly to the detective, who looked to be in charge, demanding an answer to why he had these resources out there causing such a ruckus. Fuming with anger, the mayor went directly to the detective who appeared to be in charge and demanded an answer as to why he had these resources out there, causing such a ruckus. Still furious, the mayor demanded to see, or at least hear, the evidence that they had linked the thefts to anyone in this house. The cowering detective had nothing other than, "These homeless people are thieves, thugs, and pure criminals, so we thought for sure that this was the problem. We had had no burglaries before those do-gooders hauled this scum out here." Mayor Duncan resisted the urge to slap the racist law enforcement officer right there in front of the world, but instead jotted down the name that he saw on his name badge on the lapel of his cheap sports coat.

"Okay, get your men out of here, and I'll talk to the chief about this. Go ahead, go!"

"Yes, sir." replied the stunned detective as he motioned for the crew to depart.

Reverend Don Thornton, his wife, Christina, the unofficial head of the homeless shelter project, and Jasmine, the homeless mother who now lived with the Thorntons, drove up together about when the entourage of police officers left. They went directly to the volunteer and the mayor and received a briefing on what had just occurred. Although the mayor was shocked and still spewing steam, Jasmine told them all that this was normal. This is not surprising. This is routine. People first blame the poor for everything. And if you're poor and Hispanic, or black, or Asian, you are guilty, no matter the crime. So, with eyes wide open and with an enlightened new perspective, the mayor tore away from the plantation and headed to the chief of police's home with plans to pay a visit to the judge who signed the search warrant next. These "gentlemen" were regular churchgoers, and Mayor Duncan planned a "Come to Jesus" meeting with them both.

Mayor Justin Duncan's Office

Oakdale

Monday 11:20 am

Mayor Duncan fielded calls all morning from well-meaning constituents about the robberies and how they were confident that one or more of the homeless people shipped out to the Hines Plantation were responsible. They had heard how he treated the police chief and judge for 'just investigating the crimes and making inquiries at the plantation.' They were simply doing their job, and most callers suggested he do his. Anger still existed over the number of homeless that still occupied the overpass area, and they thought that the city money spent on the homeless shelter at the Hines Plantation was to eliminate that problem. The mayor tried to reason with these irate callers by explaining that there was no room on the plantation and that he was working on an alternative plan to remove the remaining homeless from that site at the city's front door. He asked for their patience, but few were in a mood to cut the mayor any slack. "Get them out of there, or this will be your last term," seemed to be the prevailing sentiment. The mayor, a politician first, knew that something had to be done, and done fast. He called in Chris, Becky, Pastor Don, Jasmine, and members of his staff for a 2:00 pm emergency meeting. He explained to the group the increasing pressure to remove the remaining homeless people from the overpass. Early in these discussions, he reminded them that they considered using the National Guard Armory, the abandoned school, or even the now-empty tobacco warehouse. None of those options were perfect because even if they could get approval to utilize one of these sites, much work was required, which meant much money. They didn't have enough money to get the Hines Plantation up and going like they wanted. They couldn't finish the kitchen rehab because of a lack of funds. The volunteers were getting tired, and they needed paid staff. Every solution required money, and that was one scarce commodity. One suggestion popped up about using the old Sleep Tight Inn that folded when the new bypass went in. Although there was no kitchen, at least it had bathrooms, showers, and beds, and it could provide a short-term solution in that it had fifty rooms, just sitting there unoccupied. The mayor jumped at the idea and agreed to have someone on his staff investigate it to determine the current owner and the condition of the facility. If luck was on their side, they may utilize the motel at minimal expense. They all realized that nothing was that easy, and even if they could secure the use of the property, there were many obstacles to overcome to ensure that it did not turn into a haven for drug dealers, prostitutes, and who knows what else. With eyes wide open, they elected to charge full steam ahead.

Offices of McGann, Newman, and Sampson

Attorneys at Law

Oakdale Business District

Wednesday

9:30 am

Brain Newman had a full day scheduled, so he jumped right in when Becky Davis arrived at his office to discuss ways to retrieve the money that her deceased husband had stashed away in the Cayman Islands. Without the usual prolonged pleasantries, Brian began. "Becky, I've done a lot of research on using cryptocurrencies to avoid detection by the IRS. I must tell you, however, that I'm not advising this. Understood?"

"Yes, I'm with you."

"I could lose my license if I advise a client to commit tax fraud. I'm just saying that there may be a way to secure the money, not pay taxes on it, and not threaten Rick's reputation."

"Okay, I'm all ears."

"First, you create anonymous cryptocurrency wallets to ensure that transactions cannot be easily traced back to you."

"Come on, Brian, you've already lost me. What the what is a wallet?"

"Sorry, Becky. A crypto wallet is a digital tool that allows users to store, manage, and transact cryptocurrencies like Bitcoin, Ethereum, and many others. Here's how it works. Each wallet has a public key and a private key. The public key is like your bank account number, which you can share with others to receive funds. The private key is like a password or PIN, which you must keep secret. It's used to sign transactions and access your funds. So far, so good?"

"Well, yes, I guess."

"Alright, there are two types of crypto wallets: a hot wallet and a cold wallet. Hot wallets connect to the internet, including mobile apps, desktop software, and online services. Examples include Coinbase, MetaMask, and Trust Wallet. Cold wallets are offline and include hardware wallets like Ledger, Trezor, and paper wallets. These are more secure against hacking but less convenient for frequent transactions. So, once you get your wallets established, you can send and receive cryptocurrencies. When you make a transaction, the wallet uses your private key to sign in, verifying your ownership and intention. Wallets also allow you to check your balance and view your transaction history.

"Clear as mud, Brian."

Brian chuckled at the level of detail he tried to explain and knew not much would stick. But at least Becky was getting an overview that she later could use to decide. "Okay, hang in there with me. Next, you find an Offshore Exchange. Try to find one that operates in a jurisdiction with lax regulations to avoid mandatory reporting. Also, the exchange would ideally have minimum Know Your Customer (KYC) and Anti-Money Laundering (AML) requirements to maintain anonymity. After setting up the wallets and finding the right exchange, you transfer funds to the exchange. Large transfers can attract too much attention, so several small transfers would probably reduce the risk. Once the funds are in the exchange, you will buy Bitcoin. After purchasing Bitcoin, you would transfer it to your cryptocurrency wallet. This helps in maintaining control and anonymity. Easy peasy, right?"

"Brian, you lost me at 'Turn on your computer,' but I'm getting a general idea."

"Becky, please understand that there are significant risks. Many exchanges, even those offshore, are increasingly implementing KYC/AML protocols. This makes complete anonymity difficult. In addition, banks and financial institutions are required to file Suspicious Activity Reports (SARs) for transactions that appear unusual. A public ledger keeps track of Bitcoin transactions. Advanced blockchain analysis tools can trace transactions and link them back to individuals. Also, authorities are monitoring Conversion Points more than ever. Individuals convert currency to cryptocurrency and vice versa at Conversion Points. Finally, Becky, money laundering is a serious offense that could have serious legal consequences. And governments are continuously enhancing their capabilities to track and regulate crypto transactions. Becky, using intermediaries to break the money trail may increase your chances of getting away with it, but you should be aware that if you are detected, you will face consequences you are not prepared to face.

"Oh my, Brian. What a tangled web we weave, when we first practice to deceive." Becky quoted Sir Walter Scott's 1808 poem "Marmion' without realizing where the saying originated. I can tell you right now, with three young boys who have no father, I cannot, or will not take that kind of risk. I will transfer the money to an account in the U.S., pay whatever taxes are due, and hope that it does not come back to bite Rick's reputation. But he's the one who did whatever he did to generate this money, and if his reputation is ruined, it's his own fault, not mine. I'm going to use the money for a good cause, hoping the Lord will forgive him."

"Wise choice, Becky. I'm late for my next meeting, but I'll have someone on my staff contact you and get the ball rolling to get you the money and report it correctly. "

"Thanks, Brian. And thanks for the crypto lesson. I now know more than I'll ever need to know about Bitcoin."

Hines Plantation

Oakdale

Friday

8:00 am

Jesse Blackstone, the volunteer on house duty last night, felt exasperated when his replacement arrived for the day shift. "It was a heck of a night," he spewed before the replacement could barely get out a 'Good morning.' "Joe went a little crazy last night. I don't know if it was, I don't know if it was the crowded room where he slept in the old slave quarters, or more likely some kids who rode by and threw out firecrackers, but something caused him to freak out."

"What did he do?" asked the replacement volunteer.

"In his mind, he was back in Vietnam in 1969. He ran through the complex, hollering and screaming, trying to get the others to take cover. This didn't go over so well with the residents trying to sleep. He was in the bushes, crawling around the perimeter of the house, and as I tried to cajole him, with a terrified look on his face, he pulled me down with him, trying to find cover for us both. This continued for half the night before he finally returned to reality. He's in the slave quarters now, terribly sad and talking about the hopelessness of his life. With no interest in participating in any of the work around the plantation, he continues to talk about his buddies who were killed. He generally is very helpful, but not today."

We'll need to report this to Becky and Christina. He needs help much deeper than you or I can give him. Thanks for the update, and I'm sorry you had to witness that."

Becky took the news of Joe extremely hard. He had been doing so well. The doctor had prescribed Prazosin for him to reduce his nightmares, as well as both an antidepressant and an anti-anxiety medication. He either did not take the meds, or they didn't work.

The work of the plantation continued that day, however, with various residents assigned to accomplish different tasks. One managed the shower line, another removed the trash, two others watered and weeded the garden, all made their beds, and four others managed the distribution of breakfast provided by a local restaurant. Another resident prepared coffee, and they all patiently waited for the assigned person to thank God for the food before consuming breakfast. For these people to feel good about themselves, to think that they are contributing, and to prepare them for jobs and moving out to their own places, they had to relearn how to work, how to be responsible, and how to avoid drugs and alcohol. These tasks were huge steps in that direction. After completing the morning chores, they attended small group sessions led by trained counselors from local churches to discuss the issues in their hearts.

After their sessions, they were served a healthy lunch, followed by Bible study and, for some, a ride into town to follow up on referrals made by the doctor who examined every resident.

It became apparent early on that most of these folks had no medical insurance and no means to pay for medical care, much less some of the expensive tests and treatments they required. Becky insisted that one requirement to live more than a couple of nights at the plantation was that each resident must have medical insurance. After meeting with several insurance agents in town, she learned these people qualified for coverage under the Affordable Care Act, more commonly known as Obamacare. She took it upon herself to twist some arms and had two different agents spend all day at the home enlisting the residents in the plan. She was incredulous that they had not done this independently, but most were ignorant of this benefit and had no clue how to enroll. That would change. As long as the individual is a resident of North Carolina, a U.S. citizen, a U.S. national, or lawfully present in the United States, they are eligible. Becky was ecstatic to learn that North Carolina finally voted to expand Medicaid effective December 1, 2023, so most of the homeless people can receive health services like doctor's visits, emergency care, mental health services, hospital care, prescription drugs, and preventive services at little or no cost to the participants. Since it was unrealistic to expect local doctors, P.A.s, and Nurse Practitioners to give away their services, enlisting these homeless people was crucial.

Each volunteer who worked house duty expressed the sadness and helplessness they felt by having to turn down people who were desperate for a safe place to sleep, a hot shower, and something substantial to eat. Most of those turned down did not realize all the other benefits accompanying life on the plantation. They were only concerned about today, what they would eat, and where they would sleep.

Work on the kitchen had reached a screeching halt because of a lack of funds. Despite the local contractors having donated much time and resources, no one expected them to continue working for free. The work accomplished so far has helped; now, additional work is required to finish the job. The plantation needed money and needed it now. Trying to pay utilities rapidly became an issue. They needed money. Progress was being made. Success stories, albeit small, occurred every day, but the needs were significant, and the resources were small.

Oakdale United Methodist Church

Oakdale

Sunday

10:30 am

The worship service started as always, with one big difference. Clyde and Vivian Woodruff, and a few other long-time church members were nowhere to be found. In their place were three vanloads of homeless people that Pastor Don had picked up himself. The pastor saw the light when Jesus talked to him while in an unconscious state following a heart attack. The born once again pastor decided he was listening to the commands of Jesus and not Clyde or any other mere mortal. It may cause the church's demise since the homeless could offer no financial support, and the others who left carried the financial load. Those Christians who left found Pastor Don's new approach to the ministry disgusting. They questioned his faith by not pursuing disaffiliation from the United Methodist Church when the greater church was becoming more and more lax concerning same-sex marriages, openly gay ministers serving in the pulpits, and his newfound support of all those suffering in the Middle East, not just the Israelites. If taking down the American flag in the sanctuary was not enough, he now is transporting the scum of the earth to their church, the beloved church of Clyde's parents and grandparents. He just knew that his ancestors were rolling over in the graves right there on the church grounds when the church van dropped off the scraggly-looking vagrants dressed in tattered, dirty shreds of what were once clothes. Clyde donated to the soup kitchen yearly and was not opposed to helping these people. But there was no way that he wanted them at his church. So, he left.

    The collection plate carried a little over half what it usually would if Clyde and the others had been present. But Pastor Don did not let it deter him. He kept telling himself, as others expressed genuine concern, that God would provide the way. Stick to the command of Jesus regarding "the least of these," and God would see them through. "It's called faith," he said repeatedly, "Not logic." Pastor Don privately prayed that his faith, understanding of the Bible, and Jesus' words pleased the Almighty.

After church and after hauling the homeless folks back to the overpass, he managed a quick bite before heading to the plantation, where he performed a service there for those residents. For a man who almost died, who would have died had it not been for Jasmine's quick actions, he had more energy than most half his age. But truthfully, when he finally made it home at 3:45 pm, he went straight to the recliner, sipped on a decaffeinated iced tea that Jasmine had waiting for him, and dozed off for a solid thirty minutes. He was tired, but it was a good tired. He was confident that he was doing God's work and serving as the hands and feet of God. His resolve to continue had never been greater. God would provide.

Hines Plantation

Oakdale

Tuesday

7:15 pm

After being fed and taking his scheduled shower, Joe entered the family room, where several residents congregated after supper. He had had a productive day with no PTSD episodes. His anxiety and depression seemed a little better as he joked and had genuine conversations with some others. Before, at the overpass, he had kept to himself, not trusting anyone. He now appeared more relaxed. He had not yet seen a mental health professional, but the doctor who examined the residents insisted on scheduling him to see a counselor. Since he was a veteran, he was to see a counselor employed by the Veterans Administration, and they were slower to see clients than the local psychiatrists and psychologists. But he was in the cue.

Others at the home were transitioning well. One big issue that affected a surprising number of homeless people, including the Hines' residents, was foot issues. Clean socks were a cherished possession. The doctor identified Athlete's Foot, blisters, corns, calluses, foot and leg swelling (Edema), infections, ingrown toenails, plantar fasciitis, trench foot, and a more severe condition known as PAD (Peripheral Arterial Disease). Those suffering from PAD experience leg pain, ulcers, and, in severe cases, gangrene. It became clear very quickly that the feet of the homeless people at Hines required much attention and care. Since the residents all now had at least some insurance, they did not have to rely solely on the goodness of doctors. They would at least receive payment for their services, although not as much as from affluent customers with insurance. Dr. Haywood Peterson, a recently retired podiatrist, agreed to work at the plantation one day a week to improve their nagging foot problems. He was a devout Christian, so following the desires of the organizers, he started and ended each session with prayer. He bathed and soaked their feet and applied salve as necessary. Maybe as important as foot care, he listened to their stories, their aches and pains, and assessed their various levels of depression, anxiety, and other issues. Dr. Peterson referred many to more advanced medical treatments unrelated to the feet. He had a knack for getting people to open up to him, particularly when he kneeled at the feet of these lost souls. The demand grew, so Dr. Peterson, using his connections to a university medical school in the area, recruited two senior nursing students to take on the project of working one day a week, helping these people with foot issues and learning to listen. They continued after graduation, developed a training manual for washing and caring for feet, and recruited others to join them in this ministry. With the doctor's supervision, they offered minor treatments, wrote prescriptions, and referred them to other medical and mental professionals.

Dr. Peterson had his hands full when Joe entered his makeshift clinic in an outbuilding used initially for slaves to gather. Joe had Athlete's foot, corns, and a slight infection from unattended blisters and dirty, worn-thin socks. The doctor also had to cut out two ingrown toenails. He prescribed an antibiotic for the infection. When the church van made one of its regular trips from the plantation to town, Joe picked up the medication. Joe's malnutrition and an undetected heart problem caused him to develop a mild case of edema, and the podiatrist referred him to another physician for further evaluation. Joe was a model patient, very appreciative, and determined to follow the suggestions explicitly. He was becoming a success story, and the volunteers rejoiced in his progress.

Oakdale United Methodist Church

Fellowship Hall

Oakdale

Thursday 9:00 am

Christina, Jasmine, Becky, Pastor Don, and a couple of volunteers who have joined the ministry met at the church to discuss the Hines Plantation lessons learned so far in the endeavor, issues to address, and to celebrate the small victories that occurred daily. They also hoped to develop a plan to utilize the abandoned Sleep Tight Inn as a temporary shelter for the homeless folks who had no room at the plantation.

Pastor Don led with a prayer, followed by his observations. "I'm thrilled with the progress that Joe is making. He seems more relaxed and slowly participates more with the other residents."

"Yes," added Jasmine. "I've noticed the same thing. I wish that the VA would hurry and get him an appointment with a counselor to address his PSTD."

"Any progress with the kitchen?" asked a volunteer from another church.

"No," replied Christina. "We are out of funds and can't ask the contractor to give us more free labor or materials. We need to discuss this further. How are we going to raise more money?"

"Hold that thought," chimed in Pastor Don. Speaking of money, Mayor Duncan called me yesterday, and his people have tracked down the owner of the Sleep Tight Inn, and he is open to ideas about us using that facility to house some homeless. He said the facility is in fairly decent condition, but it will require a thorough cleaning, connecting utilities, and obtaining all new bed linens and towels. He will charge us a minimal rent if we keep it up, but as soon as he hears that it's turned into a drug haven or anything else shady, he will evict us. No second chances."

"Again, we need money," a dejected Chris added.

Becky spoke up for the first time. "Friends, when Rick died, he left me more money than I had expected. We have enough from life insurance, his pension from Congress, and his 401k from the medical group to live comfortably, so I donated a large sum to this effort."

"My gracious Becky," a stunned Chris said. No one expects that from you. Thank you, but I don't know if we can accept it. You have three kids, a college education, upkeep of the house, and no breadwinner for the family. I just don't feel good about this."

"It's okay, Chris. I've met with my attorney and accountant, and we all agree that I can handle it. I've prayed about it daily, and this is what I want to do, and this is what I will do. The only caveat is that I need to donate in monthly installments. But for our planning, count on $9,500 monthly for at least four years. After that, we must develop other income sources to sustain the ministry. I hope that we will not become complacent since we will have this money for four years but will go out aggressively now, developing additional sources of money. One last request regarding the money. What do you think about naming the facility 'The Congressman Rick Davis House of Hope?"

"I'm all for it," said one of the group, followed by everyone there.

"Yes, let's do it," confirmed Rick's long-time friend, Don. So, it will be."

Pastor Don broke the silence that followed her announcement with, "God bless you, Becky." With that financial support, we can finish the kitchen, buy food, pay utilities, and pursue the Sleep Tight Inn property. Praise God! By the way, I have been investigating the support available through the United Methodist Church. Suffice it to say that we have an excellent chance to receive a substantial grant from the Duke Endowment. If you please, I'll pursue that and report back to you as soon as I ferret out the details. Sometimes, it's a little bureaucratic, but I'm determined to bust through that and get what we can. We have paid our apportionments faithfully for years; now it's time to get some of that money back. I'll camp out on the lawn of the United Methodist Building in Garner if I have to."

"Yes, please, and thank you," added another volunteer.

All in attendance were smiling, uplifted, and encouraged by Becky's generosity and Pastor Don's doggedness to secure outside funds.

After the initial euphoria wore off, the group realized that there still was much to do at the meeting. But with the newfound money, the issues seemed less intimidating and more doable. Jasmine returned the meeting to reality with, "We need to recruit more volunteers. The few we have are getting burned out. I think some residents will soon be able to take on more responsibility, but we still need more people to cover house duty seven days a week."

"We seem to have a foot clinic established, but we also need to shore up our relationship with the med school to ensure that we will continue to have students here weekly to tend to the unreal amount of foot issues," said Christina.

"And I want to ensure that the group sessions continue, the Bible Study does not fizzle out, and that the Sunday service will grow and more of the residents participate," Pastor Don suggested.

Becky suggested that the group of singers that the now nine-year-old Mia leads be a part of the regular Sunday service. All loved that idea.

Jasmine added to the growing list of tasks to make this a sustainable undertaking, "There's a big need for ESL (English Second Language) teaching, GED prep, help with job applications, and for some, learning how to read and write. Someone needs to help these folks keep their doctor's appointments, get their medications, and ensure there is no backsliding with drugs or alcohol. It's a Herculean task to manage all of this."

Becky had an idea pop into her head as the group discussed all that needed to be done: "It's apparent that we need at least one paid staff member living at the plantation. I'm sorry, Congressman Rick Davis House of Hope. I can think of no one better for the job than Jasmine. She's been there, she knows the issues, she understands the medical and mental health challenges, and they respect her. With the money coming in monthly, I believe we can afford to pay her a livable wage."

Pastor Don concurred. "I agree wholeheartedly. But let me be clear: we welcome her and Mia to stay with us at the parsonage for as long as they want. It can be their permanent home if they want. She's a tremendous help to us, and let's not forget, she saved my life."

Jasmine, feeling embarrassed, could not find the right words to say. She managed to get out, "I'm not sure I can do it. I've never held a job with any real responsibility. I'm afraid I'll let you down."

Chris interrupted her, "Jasmine, you are as smart a person as anybody I know. You have just had some unfortunate circumstances cross your path, or you would be in a big job somewhere right now. You can do this, and we'll be with you all the way."

"Well, I don't plan to stay with the Thorntons forever. They have been unbelievably generous to Mia and me, but I want to be on my own. Let's pray about it and talk some more tomorrow."

"Good idea," said the pastor. "Let's all pray for it. And talking of prayer, I think we all need to soak in what transpired here today, so shall we have a closing prayer and adjourn for now?"

"Good idea."

"Pastor, please lead us in prayer."

When pastor Don concluded the prayer, the group rose enthused, with new hope and a firm resolve to make The Congressman Rick Davis House of Hope a model for other homeless shelters nationwide.

Oakdale UMC Parsonage

Oakdale

Thursday

6:15 pm

Mia has flourished since moving into the parsonage and having a stable, loving environment to live. The Thorntons bought her up-to-date clothes like the other girls in her school wear. She takes a shower daily, eats well, and has a quiet place to do her homework with three adults ready to help her anytime. Her grades improved dramatically, almost immediately after moving in. She is slowly gaining friends at school now that she looks and dresses like the others. Most of her new friends are in the choir that she joined at mid-term. The choir director noticed her talent immediately and has already had her practice a solo for the school program to be performed at the end of the term. She's never been happier.

This played heavy on Jasmine's heart as she pondered the offer to manage the "Hope House." She sincerely wanted to help these folks and believed that she was uniquely qualified to do so. Earning her own money has advantages that Jasmine has longed for ever since she found herself on the streets. A successful stint there will look good on a resume when it's time to move on to bigger and better opportunities, offering more money and better benefits. But what about Mia? Will she backslide living at the Hope House? She and her mom would have a private room and bathroom there, but is living with these people with so many mental health issues the best for a nine-year-old? Jasmine knew she couldn't live with the Thorntons forever, although they had offered just that. Jasmine just could not do that. Since Jasmine knew that Reverend Thornton could be relocated to another church in another town at any time, she knew she couldn't live with the Thorntons forever, even though they had made the offer. That decision was up to the District Superintendent and the Bishop. If the church's financial condition declines since the Woodruffs left, the bishop may bring in another minister to straighten the ship. Then what, no job and no home again?

This decision took much more prayer than she initially thought. Mia, wise way beyond her years, saw her mom struggling, praying, and stressing out. She spoke words so simple, yet insightful and perfect for her mom.

"Mom, it's been great living here. You know I love the Thorntons and all they have given us, but you need to follow your heart. That's what you always tell me. You are so happy when you come home from the plantation, knowing that you have helped someone. I think we should move out there for the rest of the school year, and if it's not working, we will find another place. As Pastor Don always says, God will provide."

Jasmine looked at her precious daughter, always shocked at her intelligence and particularly her empathy for others, and cried. "Come here, Mia, give your mama a big hug. You're the best thing that has ever happened to me in my life. I love you."

"I love you too, mama."

"We've never backed down from a challenge or an adventure. Let's do it. You and I will make this the best homeless shelter in the world. You just watch us."

So, the dye was cast. Jasmine (and Mia) Moore would take over the shelter's management with love, compassion, empathy, and energy. The Moore girls will not be stopped!

NC Conference of the United Methodist Church

Garner, NC

Friday

10:00 am

    Reverend Thornton drove to Garner unannounced to bully his way through the bureaucracy, determined to find someone to help him secure a grant (or grants) for the Hope House. Upon arriving at the sprawling three-story brick building with immaculate landscaping and a parking lot filled with over a hundred cars, he couldn't help but think of the financial struggles that his church at Oakdale and other small churches have. Is this what the money we send up here every month will maintain? Is this what Jesus wants us to do with funds raised in His name? It's a hard pill to swallow every time he rides up to this spectacular building. He walks up to the receptionist sitting behind an eight-foot counter with a ceiling that must be at least forty feet high. After introducing himself and briefly explaining what he wanted, the receptionist looked at him like he was nuts. "You drove here from Oakdale and do not know who you want to see?"

    "Yes, that's the size of it."

    "Well, let me try to help you, Reverend Thornton." The receptionist punched a few numbers on her phone, whispered to someone, and hung up. Next, she called someone else, whispering again, thanked the person on the other end, and hung up. "Hold tight, reverend," she said with a pleasant smile. I'll try someone else. After explaining her predicament, she said, "Okay, okay, sure, I understand. I'll do it. Thank you."

"Reverend Joy Martin, the District Communications Coordinator for your district, will see you. She's on the third floor in the far office to the right. The elevator is down this hall on the left."

"Thank you very much."

As pastor Don walked down the hall on the third floor, he couldn't help but glance in at all of the offices and all of the people typing on computers, talking on their phones, and scurrying about up and down the halls. "What on earth do these people do?" he thought. On his way to Joy's office, he stopped at a water fountain just as an elderly man was finishing his drink of water. To say something to the man, Pastor Don asked him, "How many people work in this building?"

The older man scratched his head, thought for a second, looked Don in the eyes, and said, "Oh, I'd say about half." With a sly grin on his face, he walked toward the elevator.

Don poked his head into Joy Martin's office to find an attractive forty-something lady pecking away at the computer. She greeted him with a big smile, offered him a seat at a small conference table in the office, and began the conversation. Joy tried her best to help him, but she had very little knowledge of the Duke Endowment or other grants available through the NC Conference of the United Methodist Church. "The lady who works with the Duke Endowment is not here. She's on maternity leave for three months," she informed the frustrated pastor. Realizing that she should give this inquisitive pastor a little more meat than she had been able to thus far, she returned to her desk, punched the keyboard on her computer, and printed a sheet to give to Pastor Don. It contained basic information regarding the Duke Endowment. She read from the sheet, giving Don a brief endowment history. "Washington Duke was a pioneering American tobacco industrialist," she read. "After serving in the Confederate Army during the Civil War, he returned to North Carolina and started a small tobacco company. In 1890, the thriving business became a part of the American Tobacco Company, which dominated the market." She continued reading, "Washington Duke's son, Buck Duke, helped to expand the family's tobacco business and played a significant role in establishing American Tobacco Company, which became a monopoly in the industry. He diversified into energy, founding Southern Power Company (now Duke Energy). In 1924, Buck Duke created The Duke Endowment with an initial gift of $40 million. His goal was to improve the quality of life in the Carolinas through support for education, health care, rural churches, and childcare."

"Finally," thought Don, "we're getting to what I came here for."

Joy read more, "Since its inception, The Duke Endowment has significantly affected the Carolinas. It has supported numerous institutions and initiatives, including hospitals, universities, and non-profit organizations. The Duke Endowment continues to honor the legacy of the Duke family by investing in and supporting initiatives that promote health, education, and human services."

"Well, Joy, what do you think? My project of housing, educating, healing, and bringing Jesus to the homeless people in my area aligns with the endowment's mission."

"It sure seems so to me. I wish I could help you more, but I don't know anyone in the building who has first-hand knowledge of the application process. Here's what I can do." She jotted down four websites that pertained to the endowment, and more importantly, she gave him the name and number of the Director of the Rural Church initiative for The Duke Endowment. This bit of information alone may have made the trip to Garner worthwhile.

"Oh wait, Pastor Don, I just thought of something. The NC Conference has just started giving out grants from the Gary Wayne Locklear Missions Endowment. Hold on, let me look it up."

"That sounds interesting."

"Here it is. The endowment has over a million dollars and issues grants up to five percent of the principal. So that's fifty thousand dollars."

"Now you're talking. What are the requirements?"

"The grants intend to support mission projects and ministries that align with the following," it says.

1. The mission-oriented projects must address community needs, promote social justice, and help marginalized populations."

"Check, check, and check," replied the excited pastor.

2. The project must align with the broader goals and mission of the N.C. Conference of the United Methodist Church."

"In other words, make disciples of Jesus Christ?"

"Yes, Pastor.

"Then, one more check."

"You must provide a detailed description of the project, including objectives, expected outcomes, and how you will use the funds."

"That's not a problem."
"Let me write down that website for you as well."

"Thank you, thank you, thank you," exclaimed Pastor Don, unable to hide his newfound enthusiasm. "Joy, you're the greatest. Thank you!"

"My pleasure, pastor. Good luck, and drive safely home."

"Will do. Bye now."

Since the Duke Endowment office is in Charlotte, Don could not go there the same day, so he headed home knowing more about the history of The Duke Endowment than he wanted. At least he found encouragement because he now had a contact who could assist him in navigating the application process and ultimately approving the church's request for support for Congressman Rick Davis House of Hope. He realized from his meeting with Joy and by reading between the lines that he should make the grant request for Duke funds through the Oakdale United Methodist Church, even though the project had grown into a community-wide undertaking. "Monday morning, I'll start working on the Reverend Dick White of The Duke Endowment," he told himself. And this news of the Locklear Endowment was almost too much to contain his excitement. Joy had brought him more hope today than he could have imagined. The narrative for that grant already swirled through his head as he headed out of the parking lot and onto the busy afternoon eastbound traffic racing home.

Oakdale United Methodist Church

Oakdale

Sunday

10:25 am

The congregation trickled in as always for the 10:30 am worship service. Christina played the piano as long-time friends greeted each other and carried on conversations throughout the sanctuary. A few heads turned when Dr. Teesa Williams, the pastor's cardiologist, walked in alongside her wife, Bess McDavid. They had visited the church twice after the heart attack, but this was the first time in a while. The bigger news, however, was revealed when behind them entered Dr. John Montgomery and his wife, along with Joyce Southern, a P.A. (Physicians' assistant) at Oakdale Hospital. This was their first time worshipping at the church.

The service went as usual, with announcements, hymns, and Joys and Concerns beginning the service. During the "Joys" period, one of the church members who also volunteered at the Hope House informed the congregation that Sleep Tight Inn was up and running. Mayor Duncan arranged for all the remaining homeless people to move into it until space opened up at the Hope House. The congregation applauded, knowing how hard so many people had worked to get this ministry to this point. Among those applauding the loudest were eighteen homeless people who now had a safe place to sleep, with a shower and a bathroom. The church lay leader, Charles Humpries, drove the church van this morning to bring the three van loads of homeless people to the service. Even Ms. Elvira, the eighty-one-year-old matriarch of the church, applauded with vigor. Pastor Don followed up by saying, "We are so blessed that God has chosen this church to lead this effort and that He has provided so many volunteers and resources to get it done. This truly is a milestone in the church's history and for the community of Oakdale. Thank you to all who have prayed, volunteered, and made generous donations to get this established." Other joys and concerns were vocalized, and then Pastor Don delivered his sermon, which focused on 2 Corinthians 5:17, where Paul writes, *"Therefore, if anyone is in Christ, the new creation has come. The old has gone, and the new is here!"* He used the butterfly analogy to talk about the transformation that occurs in our lives when we accept Christ. Just as a caterpillar undergoes a metamorphosis to become a butterfly, we, too, undergo a profound change when we embrace our new identity in Christ. A beautiful existence begins as we leave behind the old life with its sin and brokenness. He closed with this benediction. "As you go about your day, let the image of the butterfly remind you of God's transforming power and His continual provision. Just as the butterfly flies, you are meant to live a life that glorifies God, reflecting His beauty and grace.

As the people lined up to exit the church and shake hands with the pastor, all eighteen homeless people hugged the pastor, many thanking him for how he had changed their lives, not only by securing a shelter for them but by

Life Goes On

introducing them to the love of Christ. "The sermon spoke directly to me," said one homeless man with tears in his eyes. I may look the same, but I have experienced a transformation and become a new person. This heartfelt testimony made Pastor Don's eyes water as he silently thanked God for the second chance He had given him.

When Dr. Williams made it to the front of the line, she introduced the pastor to Dr. John Mongomery, his wife, and the P.A., Joyce Southern. All thanked him for the insightful sermon and pledged to be back. Joyce told him that she had looked for years for a truly inclusive church, one that followed the teachings of Jesus and one that did not fall into the temptation of becoming a social club for the rich, white people of Oakdale. "I think I have finally found my church."

The day's offering almost doubled what they had received since the Woodruffs and their money left the church. The addition of doctors and a P.A. helped.

Pastor Don and Christina left on a natural high after seeing what God was doing in the church. It may not be a miracle, like Jesus feeding five thousand people with five loaves of bread and two fish, but it was a miracle.

After a quick lunch, they were off to the Hope House for another service and looked forward to hearing Mia and her makeshift choir provide the music.

Pastor's Office

Oakdale United Methodist Church

Tuesday

9:45 am

Pastor Don answered the phone on the second ring while working on reports due to the North Carolina Conference of the United Methodist Church. He and other preachers complained about the time required to prepare all the required reports but figured that went with the job, and he strived to get it in on time. He did not want a call from the district superintendent bugging him about the past-due reports. What good the reports did for anybody anywhere was debatable, but he did not want to fight that fight. He had his orders from Jesus to get things done, and he would not waste time on a lost cause, like bucking the establishment of the United Methodist Church. It was Mayor Duncan on the line. After a few 'good mornings' and 'How's your wife' pleasantries, the mayor said what was on his mind. "Don, do you remember a while back when the police ram sacked the Hope House looking for stolen goods?"

"Sure. It seems you blew a gasket over that. The police left the place in shambles without evidence to warrant the search."

"That's the one. Well, the Police Chief just called me. They have made an arrest, and I thought that you would want to know."

"Yes, you have my interest. Who was it?"

"It's Clyde Woodruff's teenage son."

"You have got to be kidding me. Clyde's son? I remember him from Sunday School class. He seemed like a typical kid, a little impulsive maybe, and he seemed to have a sense of entitlement because of his dad and his family's status in the community, but I never thought that he was capable of this."

"There have been robberies all over town in the last few months, and the chief strongly feels he is involved in all of them. You may recall that he had a DUI arrest last year, and his dad got him off scot-free. I'm told that he is an average student at best, but Clyde and Vivian enormously pressured him to follow in his dad's footsteps. He is a risk taker, so I'm sure when someone offered him drugs, he jumped on the idea of trying them. And as you know, it's hard to stop once you start. The chief says he is a full-fledged junkie and needs extensive help and, if convicted, will probably have to serve some time, regardless of who his dad is or what high-powered lawyers he hires. It's a real shame."

"Thanks, Justin, for the heads up. Clyde did not leave the church on good terms and certainly is not a fan of my direction with the church, but I think I'll reach out to him and offer my support. He's still a long-time friend, and

I feel for him and Vivian. I see too many kids go off the deep end, but it hurts when it happens so close to home. Thanks again, Justin."

"Sure, I'll keep you posted if something else develops."

"Thank you, goodbye."

Parsonage

Oakdale United Methodist Church

Oakdale

Thursday

9:30 am

Pastor Don, Chris, and Becky gathered around the kitchen table with Chris' laptop fired up and papers covering the solid wood table. Pastor Don had talked to Reverend Dick Thomas with the Duke Endowment twice that week and clearly understood the process of applying for a grant. Reverend Thomas showed definite interest in the homeless shelter project in that it aligned congruently with the goals of the endowment, which are: 1) Health Care, 2) Children and families, 3) Rural United Methodist Churches, and 4) Higher Education. Now was the time to fill out the application and write the narrative explaining the project and its expected benefits. They wanted the narrative to show that the mission of the United Methodist

Church, "To make disciples..." came through loud and clear. So, they brainstormed. While Chris typed, they engaged in brainstorming and dictation. They read their work, added, deleted, changed, and rewrote it again. They were applying for tens of thousands of dollars, so they wanted it to be as perfect an application as they could produce. After a couple of hours, Chris read the document aloud as Don and Becky nodded in agreement. This is the final draft, and it's excellent!

Next on the agenda, after refills to their coffees, was to apply for the Gary Wayne Locklear Mission Endowment fund owned and managed by the N.C. Conference of the United Methodist Church. Fortunately, they could copy and paste much of the work done for the Duke Endowment to the Methodist application, so this one went smoothly and quickly. By lunchtime, they had completed both and agreed to allow Becky to show the work to a former staffer at her husband's congressional office who specialized in grant writing. If she had any suggestions, Chris would make the adjustments as she deemed appropriate and then submit them.

As they closed with a prayer and went their separate ways, each person fervently prayed for the approval of the grants. With almost $100,000 on the line, these grants would be a lifeline for the Hope House and its residents. They would ensure that lives would be changed, souls would be won for Christ, and the City of Oakdale would become a model for the entire state, if not the country. With high, yet guarded hopes, Chris felt a renewed sense of purpose. She was not a sought-after date for starry-eyed teenagers as she was in high school, nor was she a trophy wife for a somewhat older, charismatic minister. She made a tangible difference with her brains, energy, and Christian calling to help others. And it felt great.

Hope House

Oakdale

Saturday

10:00 am

Jasmine flourished as the Hope House Manager. She was firm, demanding, and had high expectations for each of the residents as well as the volunteers. Yet she oozed with compassion and empathy because not that many months ago, she was on the streets alongside them herself.

With Becky's donations flowing in monthly like clockwork, the team completed the kitchen, procured supplies, paid bills, and completed maintenance. Jasmine assigned each person their duties, ranging from cooking, cleaning, yard work, shopping, and laundry, and she expected all of these tasks to be completed, and on time. Surprisingly, after initially balking at the idea, the residents loved the structure and slowly fell in and did anything Jasmine asked.

Jasmine's coordination with health providers and insistence on the residents taking advantage of the plantation's benefits have led to remarkable transformations. Her goal, aligned with the founders', is to make disciples of these marginalized people, teach them responsibility, help them break their addictions, and send them into the world as productive citizens. Under Jasmine's watch, six people have already achieved this goal, and she is determined that all will follow their lead. This is the inspiring impact of the Hope House's mission, a testament to the power of compassion and dedication.

This Saturday morning started typically. The cooks prepared a breakfast of scrambled cheese eggs, air-dried sausage acquired from the "Meat Farm" in a nearby rural crossroads, grits, cheese biscuits, toast, bacon, orange juice, and coffee. After breakfast, those assigned to cleanup duty washed the dishes, took out the trash, scrubbed down the stove and counters, cleaned the coffee machine, and gathered the excess food to be delivered to the soup kitchen. The irony of a homeless shelter donating food to the soup kitchen was astounding to outsiders, but who else better understood the needs and the call of Jesus to look after the "least of these"? Jasmine made them feel special, and these residents, who came off the streets, no longer felt as though they were the least of these. They felt a sense of belonging and blessing.

Joe was cooking this Saturday, drawing on skills he learned in the Marine Corps. His cheese eggs had become legendary in the house, and he took pride and appreciated the positive comments that he received. Joe was a success story. From a loner, grumpy, homeless, and hopeless Vietnam vet, he morphed into a gregarious, Jesus-loving, positive leader of the newer residents and chipped in graciously with any chores required.

After his scheduled shower time, Joe put on a fresh set of camos, his favorite attire, and hopped in the van that took residents into town twice daily. The other riders went their separate ways when the van stopped at the corner of Main and Elm streets in the heart of downtown Oakdale. Instead, he went to a Family Dollar store and bought a couple of real-looking water guns to give to Mia and her friend. As he stuffed the toy rifles under his camos, two F-35B Lightning II Joint Strike Fighters flew overhead at a low altitude. The F-35 Bs from the Marine Corps Air Station at Cherry Point, NC, were on a training mission in and around the coastal area of N.C. Because of their low altitude and speed, they seemed to appear out of nowhere. Joe jumped from the sidewalk, crouched behind a parked car, and pulled out one of the toy water guns. Joe was no longer casually walking the streets of downtown Oakdale; he was in Vietnam in 1969. He crawled under the car, flashing the toy rifle and hollering commands to his men. He reached for his flip phone, hollering into it, "This is Alpha 1. We are troops in contact at grid coordinates Alpha Bravo 27361, taking heavy fire from the north. Requesting immediate reinforcement and CAS, over."

He "heard" back from Command. "Roger, Alpha 1. Reinforcements and CAS are en route to your location. ETA 5 minutes, over."

Joe replied to the nonexistent radio communications, "Copy that. Alpha 1 out."

In the next five minutes, while waiting for reinforcements, Joe left his position under the car and sprinted across the street, pointing his toy, but real to him, gun at shoppers and hollered, "Die gooks", a term used in a derogatory and disrespectful manner, contributing to the dehumanization of the enemy. Terrified shoppers ran into stores, ducked behind cars, and prayed. Within three minutes, three Oakdale police cars charged onto the scene, sirens blaring. In full riot gear, the brave police officers stationed themselves around the shooter and, when the opportunity arose, fired multiple rounds at the crazed shooter. No less than six rounds struck Joe in various parts of his body. The officers slowly approached the motionless body with guns drawn and pointed directly at the gunman's head. There was no movement from Joe when one officer rushed him and kicked the gun away. Another officer put two fingers on Joe's neck, held them for three to four seconds, raised his head, and informed his fellow officers, "He's dead."

Congressman Rick Davis House of Hope

Oakdale

Saturday

11:55 am

Sadness engulfed the Hope House as the news spread about Joe. Shock. Disbelief. Deep pain. Anger. Tears flowed and turned to rage as the first thought was that the police overstepped their bounds and shot first and asked questions later. Another senseless killing of an innocent black man. They were used to it, but it didn't make the pain any less real.

The department immediately placed the three police officers involved on paid administrative leave until they could conduct an investigation. Why did they shoot an innocent Vietnam veteran carrying a water gun? The initial accounts from eyewitnesses, both black and white, put a stop to those allegations quickly, with only the most radical in the town still believing that the police officers were at fault. They clearly were doing their job under the bazaar circumstances. Even though Joe had been doing so well, the sound of the jets triggered a bout with PTSD, and, to all the terrified shoppers, it was real. He had a gun, and he was going to kill people. They rejoiced upon seeing the law enforcement officers arrive so quickly and take what they believed was appropriate action.

It could have been a smell, the crowded street, or other loud noises, but the jets took him over the edge in Joe's case. His behavior was so erratic that some investigating thought that it may have been suicide. Those at the Hope House who had seen his progress and his new vigor for life squelched that idea immediately. The investigators knew that approximately seventeen veterans commit suicide every day, but Joe's death was not one of those seventeen that day.

One resident who had ridden the van with Joe that morning couldn't help but have a flashback of his own when he saw the medical crew place Joe in a body bag to be taken to the morgue. The body bag was like many that he had seen in Nam, wrapping his buddies and his fellow Marines, hauled off to centers to be flown home to loved ones. He had seen it all too often, but this one hurt as severely as any he had seen. Joe had overcome the demons, he thought, yet there he lay, dead, stuffed into a body bag.

Congressman Rick Davis House of Hope

Oakdale

Thursday

11:00 am

Pastor Don Thornton preached at Joe's funeral held at the Hope House. No blood relatives attended, and no one knew of any. There were approximately fifty extended family members present in one of the saddest funerals Pastor Don had ever preached. Doctors, medical students, nurses, residents, Jasmine, Becky, and Christina all attended with not a dry eye in the place. Two active-duty military personnel folded an American flag at the service and presented it to Jasmine, the closest person to family that he had. Another serviceman played taps at the service. After the ceremony in Oakdale, they transported Joe's body approximately forty miles to a VA National Cemetery, where the VA provided a headstone and burial, all at no cost to the "Family." Jasmine also received a Presidential Memorial Certificate signed by the President of the United States.

After the service, the residents returned to their routines, prepared lunch, ate, cleaned up, kept up with their shower schedule, and proceeded to live the best that they could.

Don, Christina, and Becky, all distraught, called Ed Murphey in Philadelphia and put him on the speakerphone. "Ed, we're heartbroken here in Oakdale and wanted to see if this has ever happened to you. The police killed a homeless Vietnam veteran, who was living in our shelter, last Saturday when he flipped out with PTSD. He was making significant progress, and some jets flying over triggered an episode, and the police shot him. No one blames the police; they did their best under the circumstances, but we've lost a resident who we thought was ready to reenter the real world."

"Sadly, this is part of the ministry that is hard to swallow. Had he accepted Christ before he died?"

"Yes, we believe that he sincerely did," answered Pastor Don. "I'm thrilled about that."

"Every day, we turn away someone in need simply because we do not have room," recalled Ed. "The joy comes when you help a homeless person find Christ. You're building relationships, not just providing food via a food line. This is good. As these people see the love of Christ in you, it helps facilitate their journey. They know you care about them and want to hear their story. Guys, this is awesome. When I was on house duty one night, a homeless person came to our home looking for a place to sleep, a shower, a bathroom, and a pair of clean socks. I declined his requests because we did not have any room. We do that every day, and it hurts. This case hurt extra hard in that I learned the next morning that this same man who asked for shelter died in the cold Philadelphia night. In his weakened state, he froze to death. I'm not over that yet, but I know there are limitations to what we can do here. The demand is great, but we have limited resources. I try to celebrate the successes and send off into the world men and women who are strong, healthy, and mentally ready to face life's challenges outside of the shelter. We can't save them all, but we sure as heck can save some. That's what keeps me going."

"I admire you, Ed, for the years that you have done this and for your continued passion," said Chris. "I am devastated right now, but I think that we all are ready to roll up our sleeves and work to save the next one."

"That's the attitude that you have to have, Chris. Don't dwell on the failures but rejoice in the successes. Keep it Christ-centered, and He will show you the way."

"Thank you, Ed, you have helped us cope today," said Becky. "I pray that we can maintain our passion as you have, and there will be many successes."

"Life goes on, my friends. Life goes on. Keep charging."

"Take care, Ed, and thank you."
"Goodbye and good luck to you all."

Congressman Rick Davis House of Hope

Oakdale

Friday

10:00 am

Someone cleaned out Joe's meager belongings from his room, finding nothing worth saving.

Based on seniority and behavior, one resident currently living in the slave quarters will now move to Joe's bunk inside the plantation home. A resident in the Sleep Tight Inn, again based on seniority and behavior, will move into the slave quarters. Although, on the surface, this did not seem to be a step up for the new resident, it indeed was. Everyone in the homeless community knew their best chance of survival was getting into the Hope House.

Jasmine gave the new resident a quick tour of the facilities and sat him down for a frank discussion of expectations. "We have zero tolerance for alcohol or illegal drugs anywhere on the premises. One offense, and you're out. We will assign you chores, maybe cooking, trash removal, yard work, or other tasks in the common area. We expect you to complete the tasks, and on time. So far, so good?"

"Yes, ma'am," replied the veteran.

We have a multitude of free services available to you; no, not available, but required of you. The foot clinic is on Thursdays in the slave gathering hall. We expect you to go every week until the staff says otherwise. The doctor and medical students are here on Tuesdays. Again, you're required to see them and follow their recommendations. A counselor will contact you through me, and you will see him or her. This is mandatory. Once you've been here a while and are ready, you'll have interviews with the people from the Employment Security Commission. We aim to prepare you for employment and for you to move to your own place. Is that your goal?"

"Yes, Ma'am."

"Now, we will add you to the shower schedule, and we expect you to take a shower every day. A barber from the Community College is here every Monday. You are to get a haircut every two weeks. We expect you to shave every day. You still with me?"

"Yes, ma'am."

"Great, now, we want you to attend the Sunday church service every Sunday here in the parlor. Reverend Don Thornton from the Oakdale United Methodist Church preaches, and my daughter and a group of residents provide the music. We pray before each meal. Finally, there is no fighting. We have zero tolerance for fighting. One fight, and you're on the streets again. Talk to the counselor if you have any pent-up anger issues, but trust me when I say, no fighting. So, what do you think? Is this a place where you can live with these rules?"

"Yes, ma'am. Since leaving the Marines, I have had no structure in my life, which is part of why I ended up on the street. I look forward to it, and I won't let you down."

"That's good to hear. Just remember, God loves you, and so do I."

Life goes on, my friends. Life goes on.

Life Goes On

ABOUT THE AUTHOR

Jeff Jenkins is a retired entrepreneur who is growing in his role as a grandpa (Pa) for three grandsons and a granddaughter.

He has three devotional books, a children's book, and two books of essays to his credit.

When not writing, he enjoys photography, winemaking, boating, traveling, chasing after his grandchildren, and exercising.

He lives with Bedie, his wife of forty-three years, along the banks of the beautiful Bath Creek in eastern North Carolina.

You can follow him at:

www.Jenkins100.com

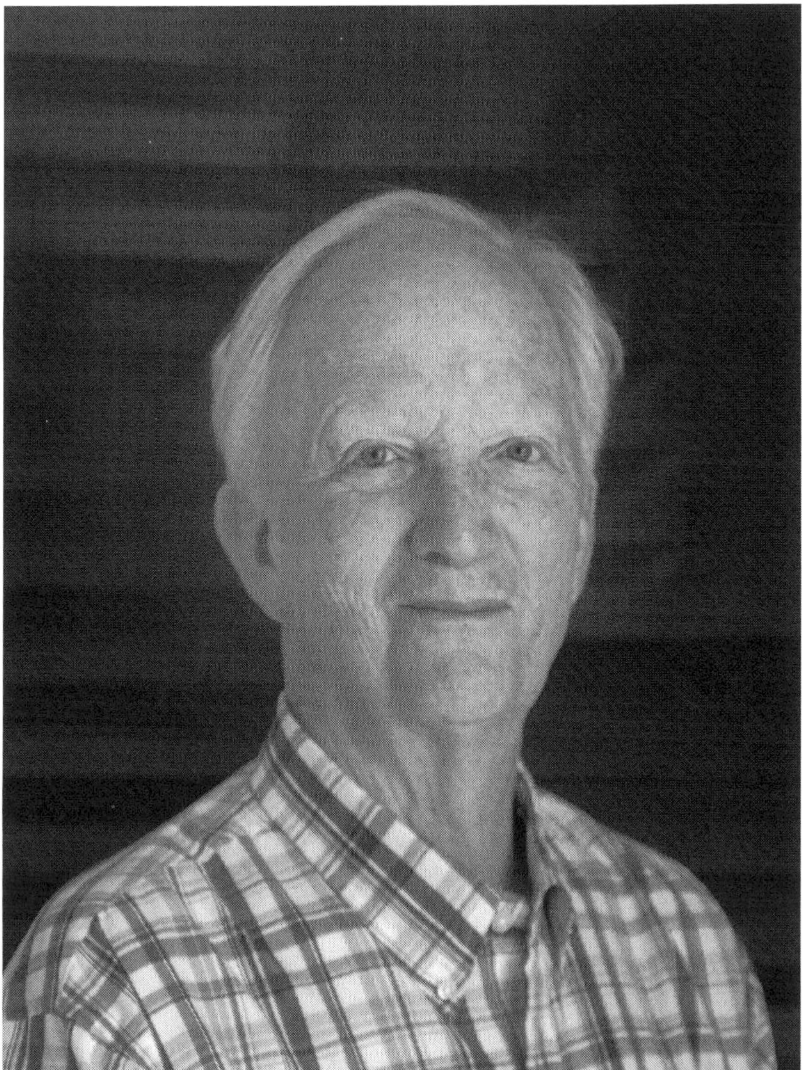

Made in the USA
Columbia, SC
01 September 2024